Anatol: A Sequence of Dialogues

Arthur Schnitzler

bibliolife
old books. new life.

ANATOL: A SEQUENCE OF DIALOGUES BY ARTHUR SCHNITZLER; PARAPHRASED FOR THE ENGLISH STAGE BY GRANVILLE BARKER

NEW YORK: MITCHELL KENNERLEY
MCMXI

Press of J. J. Little & Ives Co., New York

IT seems that in a faithful translation the peculiar charm of these dialogues will disappear. To recreate it exactly in English one must be another Schnitzler: which is absurd. This is the only excuse I can offer for my paraphrase.

H. G. B.

Anatol

I

ASK NO QUESTIONS AND YOU'LL HEAR NO STORIES

ASK NO QUESTIONS AND YOU'LL HEAR NO STORIES

ANATOL, *an idle young bachelor, lives in a charming flat in Vienna. That he has taste, besides means to indulge it, may be seen by his rooms, the furniture he buys, the pictures he hangs on the walls. And if such things indicate character, one would judge, first by the material comfort of the place and then by the impatience for new ideas which his sense of what is beautiful to live with seems to show, that though a hedonist, he is sceptical of even that easy faith. Towards dusk one afternoon he comes home bringing with him his friend* MAX. *They reach the sitting-room, talking . . .*

MAX. Well, Anatol, I envy you.

ANATOL. My dear Max!

MAX. Perfectly astonishing. I've always said it was all tricks. But he went off to sleep under my very eyes . . . and then he danced when you told him he was a ballet dancer and cried when you said his sweetheart was dead . . . and he sentenced that criminal very soundly when you'd made him a judge.

ANATOL. Didn't he?

MAX. It's wizardry!

ANATOL. We can all be wizards to some extent.

3

ANATOL

MAX. Perfectly uncanny.

ANATOL. Not more so than much else in life . . . not more uncanny than lots we've been finding out the last hundred years. If you'd suddenly proved to one of our ancestors that the world went round, he'd have turned giddy.

MAX. But this seems s u p e r - natural.

ANATOL. So must anything strange. What would a man think if he'd never seen a sunrise before, or watched the spring arrive . . . the trees and the flowers . . . and then felt himself falling in love.

MAX. Mesmerism . . .

ANATOL. Hypnotism.

MAX. Yes . . . I'll take care no one ever does it to me.

ANATOL. Where's the harm? I tell you to go to sleep. You settle down comfortably . . . off you go . . .

MAX. Then you tell me I'm a chimney-sweep, and up the chimney I go and get all over soot.

ANATOL. But, you know, it has great scientific possibilities. We're hardly on the threshold of them yet . . . worse luck.

MAX. Why worse luck?

ANATOL. I could make what I liked of the world for that fellow an hour ago. Can I shift it a jot from what it damnably is for myself?

MAX. Can't you?

ANATOL. Haven't I tried? I've stared and stared at this ring of mine, saying Sleep . . . and then wake with this little wretch that's driving you mad, gone clean from your mind.

4

MAX. Still the same little wretch?

ANATOL. Of course. I'm damned wretched.

MAX. And still suspecting her?

ANATOL. Not a bit of it. I know perfectly well that she's untrue to me. She puts her arms round my neck and kisses me, and we're happy. But all the time ... as sure as she's standing there ... I know that she's ...

MAX. Oh, nonsense!

ANATOL. Is it!

MAX. Then how do you know?

ANATOL. When I feel a thing as I feel this ... it must be true.

MAX. That's unarguable, anyhow.

ANATOL. Besides, girls of this sort always are unfaithful. It comes naturally to them ... it's a sort of instinct. Just as I have two or three books that I read at a time, they must keep two or three men hanging around.

MAX. But doesn't she love you?

ANATOL. What difference does that make?

MAX. Who's the other man?

ANATOL. How do I know? Some one has seen her in the shop. Some one has made eyes at her in the train going home.

MAX. Rubbish!

ANATOL. Why? All she wants is to have a good time without thinking about it. I ask her if she loves me. She says Yes ... and it's perfectly true. Then ... Am I the only man she loves? She says

Yes again . . . and that's true, too, for the time being.
For the time being she's forgotten the other fellow.
Besides . . . what else can a woman say? She can't
tell you. . . . No, my darling, the very moment your
back is turned . . . ! Still . . . I wish I knew for
certain.

MAX. My dear Anatol, if she really loves you . . .

ANATOL. Oh, innocent! I ask you what has that
to do with it?

MAX. A great deal, I should hope.

ANATOL. Then why am I not true to her? I really
love her, don't I?

MAX. You're a man.

ANATOL. Thank you . . . it only needed that! Of
course . . . we are men and women are different. Some!
If their mammas lock them up or if they're little
fishes. Otherwise, my dear Max, women and men are
very much alike . . . especially women. And if I swear
to one of them that she's the only woman I love, is
that lying to her . . . just because the night before
I've been saying the same thing to another?

MAX. Well . . . speak for yourself.

ANATOL. Cold-blooded, correct gentleman! I'm
afraid dear Hilda's rather less like you than she is
like me. Perhaps she isn't . . . but perhaps she is.
I'd give a lot to know. I might go on my knees
and swear I'd forgiven her already . . . but she'd
lie to me just the same. Haven't I been begged
with tears a dozen times . . . for God's sake to tell
them if I'm true. They won't say an angry word if
I'm not . . . only tell them. Then I've lied . . . calmly

and cheerfully. And quite right too. Why should I make poor women wretched? They've believed in me and been happy.

MAX. Very well, then . . .

ANATOL. But I don't believe in her and I'm not happy. Oh . . . if some one could invent a way to make these dear damnable little creatures speak the truth!

MAX. What about your hypnotism?

ANATOL. My . . . ?

MAX. Put her to sleep and draw it like a tooth.

ANATOL. I could.

MAX. What an opportunity.

ANATOL. Isn't it?

MAX. Does she love you . . . or who else is it? Where's she just been . . . where's she going? What's his name . . . ?

ANATOL. Oh, if I knew that!

MAX. But you've only to ask her . . .

ANATOL. And she must answer.

MAX. You lucky fellow!

ANATOL. Yes . . . I am. It'll be my own fault if I worry any more, won't it? She's under my thumb now, isn't she?

MAX. I say . . . I'm curious to know.

ANATOL. Why . . . d'you think she's not straight?

MAX. Oh . . . may nobody think it but you?

ANATOL. No, nobody may. When you've just found your wife in another man's arms and an old friend meets you and says Poor fellow, I'm afraid Madame isn't all that she should be . . . d'you clasp

7

ANATOL

his hand gratefully and tell him he's quite right?
No... you knock him down.

MAX. Yes... the principal task of friendship is to
foster one's friend's illusions.

ANATOL hears something.

ANATOL. Tsch!

MAX. What?

ANATOL. How well I know the sound of her!

MAX. I don't...

ANATOL. In the hall. Here she is. Well...
Hilda?

*He opens the door to find her coming in. A
personable young woman.*

HILDA. Dearest! Oh... somebody with you.

ANATOL. Only Max.

HILDA. How are you? All in the dark!

ANATOL. I like the gloaming.

HILDA. Romantic darling.

ANATOL. Dearest.

HILDA. But don't let's have any more of it. You
don't mind, do you?

*She turns up the lights and then takes off her
hat and things, and makes herself quite at
home.*

ANATOL [*under his breath*]. Isn't she...? (*praise
fails him*).

MAX [*with a shade of irony*]. She is!

HILDA. Had a nice long talk?

ANATOL. Half-an-hour.

HILDA. What about?

ANATOL. All sorts of things.

8

MAX. Hypnotism.

HILDA. You're all going mad about that.

ANATOL. Yes...

HILDA. Anatol, why don't you hypnotise me some time?

ANATOL is staggered at the sudden opportunity.

ANATOL. D'you mean it?

HILDA. Rather! Awfully jolly if y o u ' d do it, darling.

ANATOL. Much obliged.

HILDA. Not any strange person messing about of course.

ANATOL. Very well... I'll hypnotise you.

HILDA. When?

ANATOL. Now.

HILDA. Will you? Oh, how nice! What do I do?

ANATOL. Sit in that chair and go to sleep.

HILDA. That all?

He settles her on a chair, and, taking another, settles himself opposite. MAX is discreet in the background.

ANATOL. You must look at me... straight at me. And then I stroke your forehead... and then over your eyes... like this.

HILDA. What else?

ANATOL. Let yourself go.

She sits limply with her eyes shut.

HILDA. When you stroke me like that... it makes me feel funny all over.

ANATOL. Don't talk... go to sleep. You are rather sleepy.

9

HILDA. No, I'm not.

ANATOL. Just a little.

HILDA [*in tune with him*]. Yes . . . just a little.

ANATOL. Oh . . . it's so hard to keep awake. Don't try. Why . . . you can't lift up your hand.

HILDA [*tonelessly*]. No . . . I can't.

> ANATOL *makes wider passes, and his voice is wonderfully soothing.*

ANATOL. You are so sleepy . . . so sleepy . . . so very sleepy. Well, then . . . sleep, dear child, sleep . . . sleep. You can't open your eyes now.

> *It seems as if she made the most helpless effort.*

ANATOL. You can't . . . because you're asleep. Keep sleeping . . .

MAX [*really excited*]. Is she . . . ?

ANATOL. S-sh! [*Then as before.*] Sleeping . . . sleeping . . . fast asleep.

> *He stands silently for a minute looking down at* HILDA *as she sleeps. Then he turns to* MAX *and says in his ordinary tones . . .*

ANATOL. All right now.

MAX. Is she really asleep?

ANATOL. Look at her. Let her be for a minute.

> *For a minute they both watch her. Then* ANATOL *speaks again.*

ANATOL. Hilda, answer me when I ask you. What's your name?

> *Her mouth opens and the word is slowly formed.*

HILDA. Hilda.

ANATOL. Hilda . . . we're walking along a road . . . out in the country.

10

HILDA. Yes ... isn't it pretty? That's a tall tree. There's a bird singing ...

ANATOL. Hilda ... you're going to tell me the truth. Do you understand?

HILDA [*slowly again*]. I am going to tell you the truth.

ANATOL. Answer me all I ask you quite truthfully ... but when you wake up you will have forgotten. Do you understand?

HILDA. Yes.

ANATOL. Then sleep ... soundly.

Then he turns to MAX *and they look at each other triumphantly, but hesitant.*

ANATOL. How shall we begin?

MAX [*after a moment*]. How old is she?

ANATOL. She's nineteen. Hilda ... how old are you?

HILDA. Twenty-five.

MAX. Oh! [*and he dissolves into silent guffaws*].

ANATOL. Tsch! That's odd. But ... [*he brightens*] but there you are.

MAX. She never thought she'd be such a success.

ANATOL. Well ... one more martyr to science. Let's try again. Hilda, do you love me? Hilda dear ... do you love me?

HILDA. Yes.

ANATOL. There ... that's the truth.

MAX. And now for the all-important question ... is she true to you?

ANATOL *strikes the correct attitude for this.*

ANATOL. Yes. Hilda, are you ...? [*but he frowns.*] No ... that won't do.

11

MAX. Why not?

ANATOL. I can't put it that way.

MAX. It's a simple question.

ANATOL. Not at all. Are you true to me! It may mean anything.

MAX. How?

ANATOL. She might look back over her whole life. You don't suppose she never fell in love till she met me, do you?

MAX. Well . . . I should like to hear about it.

ANATOL. Would you, indeed! Prying into school-girl secrets! How was the poor child to know that one day she'd meet me?

MAX. Of course she didn't.

ANATOL. Very well, then.

MAX. So why shouldn't she tell us?

ANATOL. I don't like putting it that way, and I shan't.

MAX. What about . . . Hilda, since you've k n o w n me have you been true to me?

ANATOL. Ah, that's different. [*He faces the sleeper again.*] Hilda . . . since you've k n o w n me have you been . . . [*but again he frowns and stops*]. And it's rather worse.

MAX. Worse?

ANATOL. Think how all love affairs begin. We met quite casually. How could we tell we should one day be all in all to each other?

MAX. Of course you couldn't.

ANATOL. Very well, then. Suppose when she first

knew me she had some idle fancy still to shake free of ... am I to blame her for that?

MAX. You make better excuses than ever she could.

ANATOL. Is it fair to take such an advantage of the girl?

MAX [*with a twisty smile*]. You're a good fellow, Anatol. Try this. Hilda ... since you've loved me, have you been true to me?

ANATOL. Yes ... that's better.

MAX. Right.

> Once more ANATOL *fixes his love with a gesture.*
> *But he suddenly drops it.*

ANATOL. No, it won't do ... it won't do.

MAX. Well, really!

ANATOL. Think a minute. She's sitting in a train. A man opposite ... good-looking fellow ... slides his foot against hers. She looks up.

MAX. Well?

ANATOL. Think of the e x t r a o r d i n a r y subtlety of mind that has been engendered in her by this hypnotic trance. In her present un-conscious state the remembrance of looking up not displeased might well be recalled as an act of infidelity.

MAX. Oh, come!

ANATOL. That's perfectly sound. And the more so because she already knows my views on such a point ... which are a little exaggerated. I've often warned her not to go looking at men.

MAX. What has she said to that?

ANATOL. Oh ... asked me to imagine her doing such a thing!

MAX. Which you were imagining quite well ten minutes ago.

ANATOL. Suppose she was kissed under the mistletoe last Christmas ...

MAX. No ... really!

ANATOL. She may have been.

MAX. All this means is, that you won't ask her the question.

ANATOL. Not at all. I will ask her the question. But ...

MAX. Anatol, it won't do. Ask a woman if she's true to you and she doesn't think of men treading on her foot or kissing her under the mistletoe. Besides, if the answer's not clear, we can make her go into details.

ANATOL. I see. You've made up your mind I shall ask her, have you?

MAX. Dash it, no! It's you want to find things out ... not I.

ANATOL Yes. There's another thing to think of.

MAX. What now?

ANATOL. What about her sub-responsible self?

MAX. What the devil's that?

ANATOL. Under the stimulus of certain extraordinary circumstances, I quite believe that one is not a fully independent agent.

MAX. Would you put that into English?

ANATOL. Well ... imagine some room ... softly

curtained ... dimly lit ... glowing with warmth and colour.

MAX. Right ... I've imagined it.

ANATOL. There she sits ... she and some other man.

MAX. But what's she doing there at all?

ANATOL. That's not the point for the moment. She i s there, we'll suppose. Supper ... a glass of wine ... cigarettes ... silence. And then a whispered word or two ... ! Oh, my dear Max, colder women than she haven't stood prim against such temptation.

MAX. I should say that if you're in love with some one, you've no business to find yourself in a room like that with somebody else.

ANATOL. But I know how things will happen.

MAX. Anatol, it won't do. Here's your riddle with its answer ready. It's to be solved with a word. One question to find out if she's yours alone. One more to find out who shares her with you ... and how big is the share. You won't ask them. You suffer agonies. What wouldn't you give to know ... just to be sure. Well, here's the book open ... and you won't even turn the page. Why? Because you might find written there that a woman you're in love with is no better than you swear all women are. You don't want the truth ... you want to keep your illusions. Wake her up ... and to-morrow be content with the glorious thought that you could have found out ... only you wouldn't.

ANATOL. I ... I ...

MAX. You've been talking nonsense. It hasn't taken me in if it has you.

ANATOL. I w i l l ask her.

MAX. Will you?

ANATOL. Yes ... but not in front of you.

MAX. Why not?

ANATOL. If I'm to know the worst, I'll hear it privately. Being hurt is only half as bad as being pitied for it. I don't want your kind face to be telling me just how hard the knock is. You'll know just the same, because if she's ... if she has been ... then we've seen the last of her. But you won't be there at the awful moment. D'you mind?

MAX. Shall I wait in your bedroom?

ANATOL. Yes. It won't take a moment.

So MAX *retires, and* ANATOL *faces the sleeping girl, who is half smiling in her sleep. He braces himself for the effort, then speaks sternly, judicially.*

ANATOL. Hilda ... do you ... ?

He fails, then makes a further effort.

ANATOL. Hilda ... are you ... ?

He fails again and turns distractedly away. Then for the third time ...

ANATOL. Hilda ... have you ... ?

He begins to sweat with the emotion of it.

ANATOL. Oh, Lord! Hilda ... Hilda ...

And then, with one qualm as to whether MAX *can overhear, he throws conscience to the winds, and himself on his knees beside the pretty girl.*

16

ANATOL. Oh ... wake up, my darling, and give me a kiss.

With a couple of waves he can release her, and up she sits quite brightly.

HILDA. Have I been like that long? Where's Max?

ANATOL. Max!

Out of the bedroom comes MAX, *mischievously watchful.*

MAX. Here.

ANATOL. Yes ... a sound sleep. You've been saying things.

HILDA. Anything I shouldn't?

MAX. He's been asking you questions.

HILDA. What sort?

ANATOL. All sorts.

HILDA. And I answered them?

ANATOL [*with a look at* MAX]. Every one.

HILDA. Oh, tell me ... !

ANATOL. Aha! ... we'll try again to-morrow.

HILDA. No, we won't. You asking me what you like ... and now I can't remember any of it. I may have said the most awful things.

ANATOL. You said you loved me.

HILDA. Did I?

MAX. Who'd have thought it!

HILDA. I can say that better when I'm awake.

ANATOL. Sweetheart!

MAX. Good afternoon!

ANATOL. Going?

MAX. I must.

ANATOL. You can find your way out?

HILDA. Ta-ta.

MAX beckons to ANATOL, *who follows him to the door.*

MAX. Perhaps you've made a scientific discovery besides. That women tell lies just as well when they're asleep. But so long as you're happy ... what's the odds?

He departs, leaving the couple locked in a fond embrace.

II
A CHRISTMAS PRESENT

A CHRISTMAS PRESENT

It is Christmas Eve, about five o'clock. In a bye-street, that links up two others busy with shops, a builder's scaffold has formed a little arcade. Beneath this, and just beside a big arc lamp that sheds its whiteness down, ANATOL, hurrying along with umbrella up, meets GABRIELLE.

ANATOL [*stopping*]. Oh! How do you do?

GABRIELLE. Why, it's you!

ANATOL. What are you doing? All those parcels ... and no umbrella!

GABRIELLE. I'm trying to find a cab.

ANATOL. But it's raining.

GABRIELLE. That's the reason. I've been buying presents.

ANATOL. Let me carry some of them ... please.

GABRIELLE. It doesn't matter.

ANATOL. I insist. [*He captures one.*] But hadn't you better wait here in shelter? We shall find a cab just as quickly.

GABRIELLE. You really mustn't trouble.

ANATOL. Let me be a little attentive for once in a way.

GABRIELLE. I'll wait here a minute to see if one

21

passes. Or I'll be grateful for the umbrella. [*He tries for another parcel.*] No, I can manage that, thanks. It's not at all heavy. [*But she surrenders it.*] Oh, very well then!

ANATOL. Won't you believe that I like being polite?

GABRIELLE. As one only notices it when it's raining, and I haven't an umbrella ...

ANATOL. And it's Christmas Eve, and dark too ...! Warm weather for Christmas, isn't it?

GABRIELLE. Very. [*They take their stand looking out for a cab to pass.*] Marvellous to see you at all.

ANATOL. I've not been to call once this year ... is that what you mean?

GABRIELLE [*with much indifference*]. Oh, haven't you?

ANATOL. The fact is I've not been anywhere much. How is your husband ... and how are the dear children?

GABRIELLE. Why ask that? You don't in the least want to know.

ANATOL. You read me like a book.

GABRIELLE. It's such very large print.

ANATOL. I wish you knew more of it ... by heart.

GABRIELLE [*with a toss of her head*]. Don't say things like that.

ANATOL. They just spring from me.

GABRIELLE. Give me my parcels. I'll walk on.

ANATOL. Oh, don't be angry ... I'll be as prim and proper as you please.

GABRIELLE. There's a cab. No, it's full. Oh, dear,

shall I have to wait long? [*He is standing mum.*] Do say something.

ANATOL. I'm longing to ... but the censorship is so strict.

GABRIELLE. You can tell me your news, can't you? It's ages since we met. What are you doing now?

ANATOL. As usual ... nothing.

GABRIELLE. Nothing?

ANATOL. Rather less than nothing.

GABRIELLE. Isn't that a pity?

ANATOL. Why say that ... when you don't in the least care?

GABRIELLE. You shouldn't take that for granted.

ANATOL. If I'm wasting my life, whose fault is it? Whose, would you mind telling me?

GABRIELLE. I'd better go on. Give me my parcels.

ANATOL [*mischievously*]. I didn't imply it was any one's fault in particular. I just wanted your valuable opinion.

GABRIELLE [*with a touch of feeling*]. You idler!

ANATOL. Don't despise idlers. They're the last word in civilisation. But I'm not idling to-night. I'm as busy as you are.

GABRIELLE. What with?

ANATOL. I'm out to buy Christmas presents, too.

GABRIELLE. Are you?

ANATOL. If I could find anything worth buying. I've been looking at the shops for weeks. They haven't a notion amongst 'em.

GABRIELLE. That's what the good customer has to

supply. But, bless me! an idle person like you ought to be thinking out his presents all the summer.

ANATOL. How could I? How can I tell in the summer whom I may be making up to at Christmas? And the shops will be shut in an hour or two, and I'm still empty-handed!

GABRIELLE. Could I help?

ANATOL. Oh, you are a darling! What's my best shop?

GABRIELLE. Well, you must know that. We'll take the cab there when we find it.

ANATOL. Thank you for passing the Darling ... it's my favourite word.

GABRIELLE. I ignored it.

ANATOL. Very well ... I'm prim and proper again.

GABRIELLE. Where shall we go when the cab comes? What sort of a present? Who's it for?

ANATOL. Now ... how shall I tell you?

GABRIELLE. It's for a woman, of course.

ANATOL. Didn't I say you could read me like a book?

GABRIELLE. What sort of a woman?

ANATOL. There, again! How do you women sort yourselves out?

GABRIELLE. Is it a woman I know?

ANATOL. Not at all.

GABRIELLE. Not ... a woman I should call on?

ANATOL. Never.

GABRIELLE. No ... I thought as much.

ANATOL. Don't sneer.

GABRIELLE. You have extraordinary tastes. What's she like... pretty-pretty?

ANATOL. Pretty.

GABRIELLE. A man is a marvellous creature. Good breeding, good manners, are nothing to you!

ANATOL. Oh, a great deal ... when they'll condescend to us. But if they won't ...

GABRIELLE. Don't be silly again. No, you prefer a cheap and easy conquest!

ANATOL. I go where I'm appreciated.

GABRIELLE. Can she read you like a book?

ANATOL. God forbid. But she admires the binding, and takes the rest on trust. While you despise the contents ... as if you really knew them!

GABRIELLE. I really don't know what you mean. I can tell you of an excellent shop; I passed it just now. Cases of scent in the window. One with three sorts ... Patchouli, Jockey Club, Cherry Blossom. I'm sure that's the very thing.

ANATOL. You're unkind.

GABRIELLE. Well, there was another shop next door ... with brooches and suchlike. One with six Parisian diamonds in it ... s i x. Oh, so sparkling! Or a bracelet with charms hung round; or a long bead necklace ... quite savage! That's the sort of thing these ladies like, isn't it?

ANATOL. I'm afraid you know nothing about them.

GABRIELLE. Or I can tell you of a hat shop with a style of its own. Their bows are too large, and they put in a feather too many. These persons like to be conspicuous, don't they?

ANATOL. Not at all.

GABRIELLE. It's hard to be helpful. Make a suggestion yourself.

ANATOL. You're waiting to laugh at it.

GABRIELLE. I promise I won't. Let me know what she likes. Is she demure in sealskins?

ANATOL. I said you'd laugh.

GABRIELLE. I'm not laughing. Tell me about her.

ANATOL. I don't think I can.

GABRIELLE. Of course you can. How long have you known her?

ANATOL. Oh...

GABRIELLE. Well?

ANATOL. Ever so long.

GABRIELLE. Don't be so difficult. Tell me all about it.

ANATOL. There's nothing to tell.

GABRIELLE. What nonsense! Where did you meet her and what's she like? What's her name and her age? Is she tall or short and dark or fair?

ANATOL. It'll only bore you.

GABRIELLE. No it won't. I've always wanted to know about that sort of person... what they're really like.

ANATOL. You'll never know.

GABRIELLE. Why not?

ANATOL. As long as you fully believe that women you can't call on don't really exist at all.

GABRIELLE. But I want to learn better. And if no one dares tell me the truth ...

ANATOL [*with a sudden break of tone*]. Haven't you very virtuous ladies a feeling that this o t h e r sort of woman ... somehow gets the better of you after all?

GABRIELLE. That's a delicate insult.

ANATOL. You wouldn't change places, of course, but ... how dare she be so improperly happy?

GABRIELLE. Is it the only way then?

ANATOL. That's feminine fellow-feeling, I'm told ... and therefore all that's charming and charitable.

GABRIELLE. You've learnt to be very sarcastic since we last met.

ANATOL [*seriously, almost passionately*]. Shall I tell you how? Once I used to believe that a good woman so-called was an honest woman. I've taken a few knock-down blows with my teeth shut ...

GABRIELLE. Please don't be h e r o i c ... that's far worse!

ANATOL. Straight blows. I can take a No when it's honestly meant and said without flinching. But when the eyes say Perhaps and the smile says Wait a little, and what the No means is Yes Yes Yes ... if only I dared! Then ...

GABRIELLE [*biting her lips*]. I think I won't wait for this cab to come by ...

ANATOL. Then you've your choice between feeling a fool and becoming a cynic.

GABRIELLE. ... Unless you mean to go on telling me about ... about your new friend.

ANATOL [*back to his bantering humour*]. You simply must know, must you?

GABRIELLE. Certainly I must. How did you first meet?

ANATOL. How d o e s one meet people? In the streets, at the seaside, in an omnibus, sharing an umbrella!

GABRIELLE. Never mind how one meets p e o p l e. How did you meet her ... the Her we're finding a Christmas present for? I'm sure she's like nobody else.

ANATOL. She's just as like every other girl of her sort as you are like every other woman of yours.

GABRIELLE [*for the first time really annoyed*]. Am I indeed!

ANATOL. Oh, don't be offended. Or as I'm like every other man of mine. Are there a dozen different patterns of any of us altogether?

GABRIELLE. What's yours?

ANATOL. I, madam, am a Toy Philosopher.

GABRIELLE. And mine?

ANATOL. You are a Married Lady.

GABRIELLE. And what's s h e?

ANATOL. She? She is just a Dear Little Girl.

GABRIELLE. Then let's hear all about your Dear Little Girl.

ANATOL. It's not that she's so pretty, or so smart ... and certainly not that she's so clever.

GABRIELLE. Never mind what she's not.

ANATOL. She's as sweet as a wild flower, and as elusive as a fairy tale ... and she knows what love means.

A CHRISTMAS PRESENT

GABRIELLE. No doubt. These Dear Little Girls have every chance to learn.

ANATOL. Quite so, but you'll never learn what she's really like. For when you were a dear little girl ... of another sort ... you knew nothing at all. And now you're a married lady you think you're so worldly wise.

GABRIELLE. Not at all. I'm quite open-mouthed for your fairy tale. What sort of a castle does the princess live in?

ANATOL. Can you imagine a fairy princess in anything but the smartest of drawing-rooms?

GABRIELLE [a little tartly]. Thank you, I can.

ANATOL. Because this one lives in a little room ... with a cheap and nasty wall-paper. With a few Christmas numbers hanging about and a white shaded lamp on her table. You can see the sun set from the window over the roofs and through the chimneys. And in the spring you can almost smell the flowers in a garden across the way.

GABRIELLE. It must be a sign of great happiness ... looking forward to the spring.

ANATOL. Yes, even I feel happy now and then ... sitting with her at that window.

GABRIELLE *gives a little shiver; it's the cold, no doubt. Then ...*

GABRIELLE. It is getting late. Shall we walk on? You must buy her something. Something to hang on the nasty wall-paper and hide it a little.

ANATOL. She thinks it so pretty.

29

GABRIELLE. Why don't you refurnish the room to your taste?

ANATOL. Why should I?

GABRIELLE. With a Persian carpet, and . . .

ANATOL. No, no, no . . . She knows what she likes.

There falls a little silence.   But no cab passes.

GABRIELLE. Is she waiting for you now?

ANATOL. Sure to be.

GABRIELLE. What will she say when you come?

ANATOL. Oh . . . the right thing.

GABRIELLE. She knows your step on the stairs, doesn't she?

ANATOL. I expect so.

GABRIELLE. And goes to the door?

ANATOL. Yes.

GABRIELLE. And puts her arms round your neck, and says . . . What does she say?

ANATOL. The right thing.

GABRIELLE. What's that?

ANATOL. It's just . . . the right thing to say.

GABRIELLE. What was it yesterday?

ANATOL. It sounds nothing repeated.   I suppose it's the way that she says it.

GABRIELLE. I'll imagine that.   Tell me the words.

ANATOL. It is good to have you back again.

GABRIELLE. It is good . . . what?

ANATOL. To have you back again.

GABRIELLE. That's very beautiful.

ANATOL. You see . . . she means it.

GABRIELLE. And she lives there alone? You can always be with her?

ANATOL. She's quite alone. She has no father or mother.

GABRIELLE. And you ... are all the world to her?

ANATOL [*the cynic in him shrugs his shoulders*]. I hope so. For the moment.

There is another silence.

GABRIELLE. I'm afraid I'm getting cold standing still ... and all the cabs seem to be full.

ANATOL. I'm so sorry. I shouldn't have kept you. Let me see you home.

GABRIELLE. Yes ... they'll all be fidgeting. But what about your present?

ANATOL. Never mind, I shall find something.

GABRIELLE. Will you? But I wanted to help you buy it.

ANATOL. No, no, you mustn't trouble.

GABRIELLE. I wish I could be there when you give it her. I wish I could see that little room and that ... lucky little girl. There's a cab empty. Call it, please.

ANATOL waves to the cab.

ANATOL. Taxi!

GABRIELLE. Thank you. [*As the cab turns and she moves towards it ...*] May I send her something?

ANATOL. You?

GABRIELLE. Take her these flowers. Will you give her a message as well?

ANATOL. It's really most awfully good of you.

ANATOL

GABRIELLE. But you w i l l take them to her, and promise to give her the message?

ANATOL. Certainly.

GABRIELLE. Promise.

ANATOL [*by this he has opened the cab door*]. I promise. Why shouldn't I?

GABRIELLE. This is it...

ANATOL. Yes?

GABRIELLE. These flowers, dear little girl, are from... some one who might have been as happy as you... if she hadn't been quite such a coward! [*She gets in without his help.*] Tell him where to drive.

He does so, and then goes his way too.

III
AN EPISODE

AN EPISODE

MAX'S *rooms are comfortable, if commonplace. The writing table he is sitting at is clumsy, but it's within reach of a cheerful fire. By the lamp on it he is reading a letter.*

MAX. We're back again for three months ... you'll have seen it in the papers. Old friends first ... I'm coming along ... Your affectionate Bibi. Nice little Bianca! I shall certainly stay in.
There's a knock at the door.
MAX. Already! No, this can't be ... Come in.
In walks ANATOL, *carrying an enormous parcel.*
He looks most gloomy.
ANATOL. How are you?
MAX. What on earth have you got there?
ANATOL. This is my past.
MAX. Your w h a t?
ANATOL *deposits the parcel on the table.*
ANATOL. I have brought you my dead and buried past. I want you to take care of it for me.
MAX. Why?
ANATOL [*with great solemnity*]. May I sit down?
MAX [*as solemn as he*]. You may.
ANATOL *takes off his hat and coat and settles himself in the most comfortable chair.*

35

ANATOL. May I smoke?

MAX. Try one of these.

ANATOL *lights a cigar and unbends a trifle.*

ANATOL. I rather like these.

MAX [*pointing to the parcel*]. Well?

ANATOL. I really cannot live with my past any longer. I'm going for a holiday.

MAX. Ah!

ANATOL. I wish to begin a new life ... even if I don't go on with it. And this is naturally very much in the way.

MAX. In love again?

ANATOL. Out of love this time. So you might look after this rubbish for me.

MAX. Better burn it if it's rubbish.

ANATOL. I can't do that.

MAX. Why not?

ANATOL. This is how I'm true to them ... to all the women I've ever loved ... I never forget a single one. I have only to turn over these letters, and dead flowers, and locks of hair ... You'll have to let me come here and turn them over occasionally ... and back they come to me ... I'm in love with them all again.

MAX. This is to be a sort of Usual place at half-past three and don't be late . . . is it?

ANATOL. I've often wished there really were some Abracadabra which would call them back out of the utter nothingness.

MAX. But a variegated sort of nothingness.

ANATOL. If I knew of a word ...

MAX. Let's think of one. What about... My Only Love.

ANATOL. Yes... My Only Love! And then they'd all come. One from a little suburban villa ... one from her crowded drawing-room... one from her dressing-room at the theatre...

MAX. Several from their dressing-rooms at the theatre.

ANATOL. Several. One from a shop...

MAX. One from the arms of your successor!

ANATOL. One from the grave. One from here... one from there. Here they all are!

MAX. Would you mind not speaking the word? I somehow don't think they'd be pleasant company. I dare say they're not in love with you still... but I'm pretty sure they're still jealous of each other.

ANATOL. Wise man! Let the phantoms rest.

MAX. And where am I to put this mausoleum?

ANATOL. I'd better undo it.

He undoes it. The parcel is made up of a dozen or so other little parcels, neatly tied up and ticketed. MAX *gazes with delight.*

MAX. Hullo!

ANATOL. Yes... I'm a methodical man.

MAX. Is it done alphabetically?

ANATOL. No, there's a label for each... like the motto in a cracker. A verse or a phrase will recall the whole affair to me. No names! Susan and Jane suggest nothing.

MAX. May I look?

ANATOL. I wonder if I can still fix them all. I can't have looked at some of them for years.

> ANATOL *leans back in his chair, smoking.* MAX *settles himself enjoyably to the Past. He takes up the first packet and reads the motto.*

MAX. ' I loved her. When she left me I thought
    I should have killed her;
    My kisses on your neck remain, and nothing
    else, Matilda.'
But that's a name ... what a name! Matilda!

ANATOL. It wasn't her real name, but I'd written ' killed her,' and there aren't many rhymes to that. I always did kiss her on the neck, though.

MAX. Who was she?

ANATOL. It doesn't matter. I held her in my arms once. That's all there is to her.

MAX [*as he puts the packet aside*]. Stand down, Matilda. She does up small, anyhow.

ANATOL. One lock of hair.

MAX. No letters?

ANATOL. Letters from Matilda! That would have inked her fingers. Don't you sometimes wish women weren't taught to write? Exit Matilda.

> MAX *reads another label.*

MAX. ' Women are alike in one thing ... they turn impudent if you catch them out in a lie.'

ANATOL. They do.

MAX. Who was it? She's very heavy.

ANATOL. Lies eight pages long. Oh ... put it away.

MAX. Was she so very impudent?

ANATOL. When I found her out. Throw her away.

MAX. Impudent little liar!

ANATOL. No... you mustn't insult her. I have held her in my arms. She is sacred.

MAX. How stupid of me! Who's next? [*A third packet.*]

> 'When sad, my child, and sick of earth,
>> My thoughts to your Young Man fly far,
>> And then I laugh for all I'm worth;
>> Oh, dear, how funny some things are!'

ANATOL. So they were!

MAX. What's inside?

ANATOL. A photograph. She and the Young Man.

MAX. Did you know him, too?

ANATOL. That's what was so funny. He really was quite an exceptional fool.

MAX. Hush! She has held him in her arms ... he is sacred.

ANATOL. You shut up.

MAX. Stand down, my child, with your exceptionally foolish and mirth-provoking young man. [*With a fourth package.*] What's this?

ANATOL. What?

MAX. 'A box on the ears.'

ANATOL. Oh ... ! Oh, yes ... yes ... yes!

MAX. Was that how it ended?

ANATOL. No, how it began.

MAX. Ah! [*A fifth label.*] 'How hard it is to

grow a flower, but it's so easy to pick it.' What does that mean?

ANATOL. Some other fellow grew the flower... I came along and picked it.

MAX. Oh! [*A sixth label.*] 'She always carried her curling tongs.'

ANATOL. Do you know she always did. Then it didn't matter what happened. I tell you ... she was damn pretty. There's a bit of her veil left, isn't there?

MAX. It feels like that. [*A seventh label.*] 'How did I lose you?' How did you lose her?

ANATOL. That's the point ... I never knew. One fine day she just wasn't. Don't you know how you leave your umbrella somewhere ... don't think of it till days later ... no idea where you put it down.

MAX. Fare thee well, my lost umbrella! [*An eighth label.*] What's this one? 'Sweet and dear you were to me ...'

ANATOL [*catching him up*]. 'Girl with roughened finger tips. Past all ...'

MAX. Oh ... that was Hilda.

ANATOL. You remember Hilda.

MAX. What became of her?

ANATOL. She married a milkman.

MAX. Did she now?

ANATOL. That's what happens. I love a girl ... I'm all the world to her ... and then she marries a milkman. A dear child. I hope it's been good for trade.

MAX [*as he puts* HILDA *aside*]. Milko! [*Then the*

AN EPISODE

ninth package.] And what's 'Episode'? Nothing inside but a little dust.

ANATOL *leans across and takes the little envelope from him.*

ANATOL. Dust! It was once a rosebud.

MAX. What does 'Episode' mean?

ANATOL. That's what it was... an episode... a couple of hours' romance. Pathetic, isn't it? Nothing left of its sweetness but dust!

MAX. Most pathetic. But one might call them all a little episodic.

ANATOL. Not with such dreadful truth. Of course, they all were... and I knew they were at the time. I had a fine idea of myself in those days. I used to catch myself thinking... Poor child, poor child!

MAX. Poor...?

ANATOL. When I was very young indeed I saw myself as one of the world's great heroes of romance. These women, I thought... I pluck them, crush the sweetness from them . . . it's the law of nature . . . then I throw them aside as I pass on. I know now that I'm more of a fool than a hero... and I'm getting most unpleasantly used to knowing it.

MAX. What was 'Episode'?

ANATOL. I caught her . . . then I threw her aside ... crushed her under my heel.

MAX. Did you really?

ANATOL. But I tell you... they were the few most wonderful moments I ever passed. Not that you'd ever understand.

41

ANATOL

MAX. Why not?

ANATOL. Because it sounds nothing at all ...
unless you can feel it as I felt it.

MAX. I'll try.

ANATOL. I sat at the piano in that room of mine
one evening. We'd been in love with each other
just two hours. D'you remember a lamp I had and
the curious glowing light it gave. Think of that
lamp ... it's most important.

MAX. I've thought of it.

ANATOL. I sat at the piano. She sat at my
feet ... I remember I couldn't reach the pedals.
Her head in my lap ... her hair loose ... and the
glowing light making such shadows in it! I let one
hand wander on the keys ... the other was pressed
against her lips.

MAX. What e l s e ?

ANATOL. Isn't that like you? Nothing e l s e !
We'd loved each other for only an hour or two.
It was our first solitude ... it was to be our last. She
said it would be. But I knew that she loved me
madly ... the very air was shimmering with it.
Would you have noticed that? Do you wonder I felt
a demi-god and only thought ... Oh, you poor, poor
child! What was it to me? An episode. I should
hardly cease to feel her kisses on my hand before
she'd begin to slip into the shadows of memory.
But she'd never forget ... never be able to forget.
Some women can ... but not she. She lay there at
my feet pouring out her soul in love. I knew that
I was the whole world to her ... and always would

42

be . . . one is so certain of these things sometimes.
While to me . . . she and her love were just an
episode.

MAX. Who was the lady?

ANATOL. You knew her . . . we met her at supper
once.

MAX. Did we? Sounds too romantic a person for
any supper I ever went to.

ANATOL. Not a bit. You'll laugh when I tell
you. She belonged to a . . .

MAX. Theatre?

ANATOL. No . . . a circus.

MAX. Not Bianca?

ANATOL. Yes . . . Bianca. I never told you I met
her again after that night.

MAX. D'you mean to say that Bibi was in love
with you?

ANATOL. She was. I met her in the street . . . it
seems they went off to Russia the next morning.

MAX. And a good job for your romance they did.

ANATOL. Of course! Because it's somebody you
knew the whole thing becomes commonplace. Oh,
Max . . . why don't you learn how to be in love?

MAX. Teach me.

ANATOL. Learn to tune yourself up to the supreme
moments.

MAX. With a little piano-playing and a glowing
light upon her shimmering hair?

ANATOL. Well . . . that's how I get wonders out of
life. You saw no more in that girl than you could
in that lamp of mine. A bit of glass, wasn't it . . .

with a light behind? What a way to walk through the world ... eyes open and imagination shut! Do you wonder you find nothing in it? You swallow life whole, Max ... I taste it.

MAX. You've only to fall in love to make the universe all you want it to be!

ANATOL. That's how it's done

MAX. How many glowing lamps would it take to work Bianca up to that pitch?

ANATOL. I know what she felt when I kissed her.

MAX. I know better.

ANATOL. Do you?

MAX. Because I've never kissed her ... and never needed to imagine her anything but the pretty, harmless, worthless little baggage she is.

ANATOL. Oh!

MAX. Whatever else you want to find in her you must put there first.

ANATOL. It wasn't so then ... it wasn't. Oh ... I know all about the girl. She'd kissed men before, and she has kissed them since.

MAX. With just the same kisses that she kissed you.

ANATOL. No. I wish I hadn't told you.

MAX. Never mind. You felt all you felt and all she ought to have felt as well.

ANATOL. Have you ever seen much of her?

MAX. Quite a lot.

ANATOL. Have you?

MAX. Don't distress yourself. She's a witty little devil, and we always liked a chat.

ANATOL. A friendly chat?

44

AN EPISODE

MAX. Not a bit more.

ANATOL. Then I swear to you, Max... that girl loved me to distraction.

MAX. Quite so. Let's get on with the others [*he takes a tenth packet*]. 'Could I but tell the meaning of your smile, you green-eyed'...

ANATOL. I say... d'you know that circus is back again?

MAX. Yes... she's still with it.

ANATOL. Sure?

MAX. Quite. I shall see her this evening... she's coming to call.

ANATOL. Well! Why on earth didn't you tell me that before?

MAX. What's it to do with you? Your past is dead... look at it.

ANATOL. But...

MAX. Besides... yesterday's romance warmed up. Don't risk that.

ANATOL. I wonder if I could feel the same for her again.

MAX. There are other dangers. You take great care of this Episode of yours. Don't let it catch cold.

ANATOL. But I mustn't miss a chance of seeing her.

MAX. She's wiser than you! Has she ever sent you even a postcard? But perhaps she forgot all about you.

ANATOL. Max... why not believe me when I tell you...?

MAX. Well?

45

ANATOL. That the hour we spent together was one of those things that never fade.

There's a knock at the door of the flat.

MAX. Here she is!

ANATOL. What!

MAX. You go into my bedroom and then slip out.

ANATOL. Certainly not.

MAX. You'd much better.

ANATOL. I shall not.

MAX. Stand there then, where she won't see you at once.

ANATOL. But why...?

Still, he stands in the shadow, and MAX *goes to the door to welcome* BIANCA. *She is as he described her.*

BIANCA. Max! How are you? I'm back.

MAX. How are you, Bibi? Nice of you to come.

BIANCA. First visit.

MAX. Honoured.

BIANCA. How's everybody? Suppers at Sacher's again now?

MAX. But you must turn up. Sometimes you didn't.

BIANCA. I did.

MAX. Not when you'd something better to do.

BIANCA. But you weren't jealous. I wish they'd all take lessons from you. Why can't a man be fond of one without making himself a nuisance?. Oh... who's that? Making one jump!

She has discovered ANATOL, *who comes forward, silent, expectant. She stares at him.*

AN EPISODE

MAX. An old friend, Bibi.

BIANCA. Oh . . .

MAX. Quite a surprise.

> ANATOL *comes nearer.* BIANCA *is desperately*
> *puzzled. She doesn't recall him in the least*
> *She is most polite.*

BIANCA. Of course . . . we've met . . .

ANATOL. Bianca.

BIANCA. Yes . . . to be sure.

> ANATOL *seizes her hand quite passionately.*

ANATOL. Bianca.

BIANCA. But . . . I'm so stupid . . . where was it?

MAX. Try hard to remember.

BIANCA. Of course . . . in Petersburg.

ANATOL. No . . . it wasn't in Petersburg.

> *With that he drops her hand, takes his hat and*
> *coat and goes.*

BIANCA. Oh . . .

> *The flat door slams.*

MAX. He's gone.

BIANCA. But . . . I'm so sorry . . . what's wrong . . . ?

MAX. Don't you really remember him?

BIANCA. Yes . . . quite well. But I can't place him
for the life of me.

MAX. Anatol, Bibi . . . Anatol.

BIANCA [*her brow wrinkling in puzzlement*]. Anatol . . . Anatol?

MAX. Anatol . . . at the piano . . . and a lamp
casting shadows on your shimmering hair. Here . . .
not in Petersburg . . . three years ago.

> *A light breaks on* BIANCA.

47

BIANCA. Well . . . of course . . . Anatol! How stupid of me. Oh, do call him back. Anatol!

She makes for the door.

MAX. No . . . he's gone.

She looks from the window.

BIANCA. There he goes.

MAX [*behind her*]. Yes . . . there he goes.

BIANCA [*calling*]. Anatol!

MAX. No use . . . he can't hear.

BIANCA. You will apologise to him, won't you? I've hurt his feelings. Such a nice fellow.

MAX. You're quite sure you remember him?

BIANCA. Why, yes! But, you know, there is some one in Petersburg as like him as two peas.

MAX. I'll tell him so.

BIANCA. Besides . . . when you haven't given a man a thought for three years . . . and there he suddenly is plumped in front of you! One can't remember everybody.

MAX [*grimly smiling*]. Let's shut the window . . . it's gone chilly.

BIANCA. I shall run against him somehow.

MAX. No doubt [*he picks up and holds out to her the little envelope marked ' Episode '*]. D'you know what this is?

BIANCA. What?

MAX. The rosebud you were wearing that evening . . . t h e evening, Bibi . . .

BIANCA. Has he kept it?

MAX. As you see.

BIANCA. D'you mean he was in l o v e with me?

48

MAX. Passionately . . . unfathomably . . . and for ever and a day. But so he was with all these others.

BIANCA *surveys the table full.*

BIANCA. All that lot!

MAX. We've been sorting you out.

BIANCA. Sorting us . . . ?

MAX. Sorting you.

BIANCA. Oh, indeed! Where do I go?

MAX. Here.

He gravely drops 'Episode' in the fire.

BIANCA. Well!

MAX. All the revenge I can give him you see. But don't be cross . . . I want to hear your news.

BIANCA. I don't think I feel like it now.

MAX. Bibi . . . don't quarrel with m e. Let's hear about the fellow in Petersburg, who's as like him as two peas.

BIANCA. Don't be absurd.

MAX. Or anything else you like. I'll tell you how to begin.

He settles her in a big armchair, and settles himself in another beside her.

MAX. Once upon a time there was a big, big city . . .

BIANCA . . . And into the city came a big, big circus . . .

MAX. . . . And in the circus there was a tiny, tiny girl . . .

BIANCA. . . . Who jumped through a big, big hoop.

49

MAX. Now we're getting on. And in a box every evening . . .

BIANCA. Yes . . . in a box every evening there sat a very good-looking man . . .

MAX. Quite so . . . and then?

They settle to their friendly chat.

IV

KEEPSAKES

KEEPSAKES

EMILY'S *sitting-room is quite prettily furnished, and looks over some gardens, where the trees are just now breaking into leaf. It is late in the afternoon. Alone in the room and at the writing-desk sits* ANATOL. *He is feverishly searching the drawers.* EMILY *comes in and finds him.*

EMILY. What are you doing at my desk... rummaging about? Anatol!

> *He hardly looks up even.*

ANATOL. I have a perfect right to. And it's as well I did.

EMILY. What have you found ... except your own letters?

ANATOL. My letters! What do you call these?

> *Two tiny objects which he had placed safely on the top of the desk. He shows them to her in his outstretched palm.*

EMILY. What?

ANATOL. These two stones. This one's a ruby ... and this other dark one. I've never seen them before. I didn't give them you.

> EMILY *turns away, and for a moment doesn't answer. When she does it is very quietly.*

EMILY. No ... I had quite forgotten them.

53

ANATOL [*still brutally, sneeringly angry*]. Had
you! They were hidden away safe enough in the bot-
tom of that drawer. Come on ... you'd better confess. Don't lie. Oh, all you women do! Won't you?
Don't pretend to be indignant. Yes, of course ... sulk
when you're found out. I want to know what else there
is. Where have you hidden your other treasures?

He returns to his ransacking.

EMILY. I haven't any others.

ANATOL. Haven't you?

EMILY [*quite passive*]. You needn't look. I
swear I haven't.

ANATOL. Well then ... what about these?

EMILY. I suppose I was wrong. I shouldn't have ...

He leaves the desk and faces her.

ANATOL. You suppose! Now Emily ... to-morrow
we were to be married. I thought we'd got rid of
the past ... utterly. Didn't I bring you everything
I had that could remind me of mine ... letters, keep-
sakes, everything ... and didn't we burn them? And
your rings and bracelets and earrings! Haven't we
got rid of them too ... all of them? Given them
away ... thrown them into the river ... out of the
window ... anywhere? And you s w o r e to me that
you had done with it all ... wiped everything out!
You said that n o w you knew you'd never really been
in love with any one before. And I believed you! I
suppose we always do believe women when the lies
are pleasant ones ... from their first lie to their last
... because we want to.

EMILY. Shall I swear it again?

54

KEEPSAKES

ANATOL. What's the good? I've done with you ...
done with you. Oh, you were very clever about it!
To see you standing there in front of the fire watching those letters and things burn ... poking them
down so that nothing should escape ... wouldn't one
have thought you were only thankful to be rid of
every speck of your past? You sobbed in my arms
that day by the river when we threw that bracelet
into the water! Tears of repentance? All a sham!
Now I'll tell you ... I d i d n ' t trust you in spite
of them. I came here to find out for myself ... and
I have found out. [*She is sitting silent, her head
away.*] Say something. Defend yourself.

EMILY. No ... you've made up your mind to have
done with me.

ANATOL. But I want to know about these two
things. Why keep just t h e s e two?

EMILY. You don't love me any more.

ANATOL. Emily ... I want to know the truth.

EMILY. What's the good if you don't love me any
more?

ANATOL. Tell me the truth. Perhaps ...

EMILY. Well?

ANATOL. Perhaps you can make things seem a bit
better. I don't want to think badly of you, Emily.
She turns a little towards him.

EMILY. D'you forgive me?

ANATOL. Tell me the truth.

EMILY. If I do ... will you forgive me?
*He doesn't answer for a moment. Then his
voice half hardens again.*

55

ANATOL. This ruby! What about it...why have you kept it?

EMILY. Will you be patient?

ANATOL. Yes...yes. Go on.

After a moment she does, speaking quite tone-lessly, her head bent.

EMILY. It came out of a locket It fell out.

ANATOL. Who gave you the locket?

EMILY. Oh...that wasn't it. It was because of ...the day I was wearing it.

ANATOL. But who gave it you?

EMILY. What does it matter? My mother, I think. Oh, Anatol...if I were the bad lot you think me, I could easily say I kept the stone because my mother gave it me. You'd believe that I kept it because I didn't want ever to forget that day I nearly lost it.

ANATOL. Go on.

EMILY. I am so glad to be telling you. But listen now. You'd laugh at my being jealous of the first woman you were ever in love with, wouldn't you?

ANATOL. What's that to do with it?

EMILY. But I dare say you're still in love with the memory of her. It's the sort of old unhappiness one never wants quite to lose, isn't it? The day I dropped that ruby means a lot to me, because it was the day I had my first glimpse of... everything that you and I can mean to each other now, if we will. Oh...if I'd never had to learn how to love... d'you think I could love you as I do? Anatol...if

we'd met t h e n . . . before we knew what love meant
. . . should we have given each other a thought?
Don't shake your head. You once said that to me
yourself.

ANATOL. I did.

EMILY. You told me not to be so sorry that things
were . . . as they were . . . because if we hadn't both
learnt by experience, we could never love each other
as we do.

ANATOL [*bitterly*]. Yes . . . that's all the consola-
tion one has in loving a woman who . . . [*he swallows
the insult*] oh, never mind!

EMILY [*with dignity*]. I'm telling you the truth
about this. I kept it to remind me of the day
that . . .

ANATOL. Say the words!

EMILY. You like to humiliate me. It was the very
first time that . . . I was just a silly girl. What
was I . . . sixteen?

ANATOL. He was twenty . . . and tall and dark . . .
I'm sure.

EMILY [*quite simply*]. D'you know I don't remember, dear. I remember the wood we were in, and the
wind shaking the trees. It was in the spring. Yes
. . . and the sun shone through the branches and made
the primroses look so bright.

ANATOL *paces the room with a sudden access of
fury.*

ANATOL. And you were stolen from me before I
ever knew you! Don't you hate him . . . the very
thought of him?

EMILY. Perhaps he gave me to you, Anatol. [*That brings him to a stand.*] No ... whatever happens I don't hate the thought of him ... I won't pretend I ever did. Don't you know I love you as I have never loved any one? And no one has ever loved you as I love you. But in spite of that ... and even though when you kissed me first you made me forget every one else ... all I'd ever gone through ... wiped it out utterly ... you can't make me forget, and you can't make me regret the moments that made me a woman.

ANATOL. You love m e , do you?

EMILY. I hardly remember what he looked like ... or anything he said.

ANATOL. Only that he kissed you ... held you close to him ... turned your ignorance into knowledge and your innocence into guilt. And you're grateful for that ... grateful! Good God ... can't you see what this means to me ... stirring up again all this horrible past when I'd almost forgotten that there ever was or could be any other man in the world for you but me.

> She looks at him and then speaks with a certain
> cold sadness.

EMILY. Yes ... you don't understand. I think you were right. We'd better part.

ANATOL [*not quite prepared for this*]. What else d'you expect of me?

EMILY [*emotional for the first time*]. I envy a woman who can lie. It's a costly business telling the truth. But there's one thing I'd like to know.

Why you have always begged me to be quite
straight with you. How many times have you said
that there was nothing you couldn't forgive me
except a lie. So I confessed everything to you ...
and never cared how bad I made myself out. I told
you that the only good thing about me was my love
for you. Any other woman would have made excuses ... I didn't. I let you know that I was vain
and wanton ... that I'd wasted and sold myself ...
that I wasn't worth your loving. I told you that
before I'd let you come near me. I hid away from
you, didn't I? It was just because I loved you so.
You found me and you cried for me. But I still said
No. I didn't want to drag you down ... although
your love meant more to me than anything else had
ever meant in the world. I've never loved any one
but you. In spite of everything you took me. I
was so glad and so afraid! But why have you given
me back bit by bit all the beauty and self-respect
that the others had robbed me of ... why have you
made me innocent again by being great enough to
be able to forgive ... if now ... ?

ANATOL [*echoing her as she pauses*]. Now?

EMILY. If now you're done with me only because I
am just like all the others?

ANATOL. No, no, dear ... you're not, you're not.

EMILY. What do you want me to do then? Shall
I throw it away?

She fingers the little ruby disdainfully.

ANATOL [*passionately self-reproachful*]. What is
there great about me? I'm worse than human.

59

ANATOL

Yes .. throw it away. You dropped it, did you, among the primroses ... and it glittered in the sun ...

> *They sit there silently; the poor little trinket on the table between them. Then he rouses.*

ANATOL. It's dark ... let's go out.

EMILY. It'll be so cold.

ANATOL. No ... you can feel the Spring's in the air.

EMILY. Very well, darling.

> *She moves, and as he moves too his eye lights on the other stone he had found*

ANATOL. But what about t h i s one?

EMILY. That?

ANATOL. Yes, the black stone ... what about that?

> *She takes it up with care.*

EMILY. Don't you know what it is?

ANATOL. It looks like a ...

EMILY. It's a black diamond!

> *Her eyes glitter as she holds it.*

ANATOL. What?

EMILY. They're very scarce.

ANATOL [*hardly articulate*]. Why ... have you kept it?

EMILY. It's worth a hundred pounds!

ANATOL. Ah!

> *He snatches the stone from her and throws it into the fire. She shrieks out savagely ...*

KEEPSAKES

EMILY. What are you doing?

Then throws herself on her knees and snatching up the tongs does her best to rescue it. He watches her grimly for a little; the firelight makes ugly shadows on her face. Then he says quietly . . .

ANATOL. That was your price, was it?

And he leaves her.

V

A FAREWELL SUPPER

A FAREWELL SUPPER

*In a private room at Sacher's restaurant one evening,
about supper-time, we find* ANATOL *and* MAX.
MAX *is comfortable upon a sofa with a cigarette.*
ANATOL *stands by the door discussing the menu
with the waiter.*

MAX. Haven't you done?

ANATOL. Just.   Don't forget now.
  This to the waiter, who disappears. ANATOL
    begins to pace the room, nervously.

MAX. Suppose she don't turn up after all.

ANATOL. It's only ten.   She couldn't be here yet.

MAX. The ballet must be over long ago.

ANATOL. Give her time to take her paint off and
dress.   Shall I go over and wait for her?

MAX. Don't spoil the girl.

ANATOL [*mirthlessly laughing*]. Spoil her...
spoil her!

MAX. I know... you behave like a brute to her.
Well... that's one way of spoiling a woman.

ANATOL. No doubt. [*Then, suddenly stopping
before his friend.*] But, my dear Max... when I
tell you... oh, Lord!

MAX. Well?

ANATOL. ... What a c r i t i c a l evening this is!

MAX. Critical! Have you asked her to marry you?

ANATOL. Worse than that.

MAX [*sitting up very straight*]. You've married her? Well!

ANATOL. What a Philistine you are. When will you learn that there are spiritual crises besides which such commonplace matters as ...

MAX [*subsiding again*]. We know! If you've only got one of those on I wouldn't worry her with it.

ANATOL [*grimly*]. Wouldn't you? What makes this evening critical, my friend, is that it's to be the last.

MAX [*sitting up again*]. What?

ANATOL. Yes ... our farewell supper.

MAX. What am I doing at it?

ANATOL. You are to be the undertaker ... to our dead love.

MAX. Thank you! I shall have a pleasant evening.

ANATOL. All the week I've been putting it off.

MAX. You should be hungry enough for it by this time.

ANATOL. Oh, we've had supper every night. But I've never known how to begin ... the right words to use. I tell you ... it's nervous work.

MAX. If you expect me to prompt you ...

ANATOL. I expect you to stand by me. Smooth things down ... keep her quiet ... explain.

MAX. Then suppose you explain first.

ANATOL *considers for half a second. Then ...*

ANATOL. She bores me.

MAX. I see! And there's another she ... who doesn't?

ANATOL. Yes.

MAX [*with fullest comprehension*]. Ah!

ANATOL [*quite rapturously*]. And what another!

MAX. Please describe her.

ANATOL. She makes me feel as I've never felt before. She ... I can't describe her.

MAX. No ... one never can till it's all over.

ANATOL. She's a little girl that ... well, she's an andante of a girl.

MAX. Not out of the ballet again?

ANATOL. No, no! She's like a waltz ... simple, alluring, dreamy. Yes, that's what she's like. Don't you know ... ? No, of course you don't! And how can I explain? When I'm with her I find I grow simple too. If I take her a bunch of violets ... the tears come into her eyes.

MAX. Try her with some diamonds.

ANATOL. I knew you wouldn't understand in the least. I should no more think of bringing her to a place like this ... ! Those little eighteenpenny places suit her. You know ... Soup or Fish: Entrée: Sweets o r Cheese. We've been to one every night this week.

MAX. You said you'd had supper with Mimi.

ANATOL. So I have. Two suppers every night this week! One with the girl I want to win, and the other with the girl I want to lose. And I haven't done either yet.

MAX. Suppose you take Mimi to the Soup o r Fish,

and bring the little Andante girl here. That might do it.

ANATOL. That shows you don't understand. Such a child! If you'd seen her face when I ordered a one and tenpenny bottle of wine.

MAX. Tears in her eyes?

ANATOL. She wouldn't let me.

MAX. What have you been drinking?

ANATOL. Shilling claret before ten. After ten, champagne. Such is life.

MAX. Y o u r life!

ANATOL. But I've had enough of it. To a man with my nice sense of honour ... my nice sense of honour, Max.

MAX. I heard.

ANATOL. If I go on like this much longer I shall lose my self-respect.

MAX. So shall I if I have much more to do with you.

ANATOL. How can I play-act at love if I don't feel it?

MAX. No doubt it's better acting when you do.

ANATOL. I remember telling Mimi in so many words ... when we first met ... when we swore that nothing should part us ... My dear, I said, whichever first discovers that the thing is wearing thin must tell the other one straight out.

MAX. Besides swearing that nothing should part you. Good!

ANATOL. If I've said that once I've said it fifty times. We are perfectly free, and when the

time comes we'll go each our own way without
any fuss. Only remember, I said, what I can't stand
is deceit.

MAX. Then I'm sure supper ought to go off very
well.

ANATOL. Yes . . . but when it comes to the point . . .
somehow I can't tell her. She'll cry. I know she'll
cry, and I can't bear that. Suppose she cries and I
fall in love with her again . . . then it won't be fair to
the other one.

MAX. And the one thing you can't stand is deceit.

ANATOL. It'll be easier with you here. There's an
honest, unromantic air about you that would dry any
tears.

MAX. Happy to oblige. And how shall I
start? Tell her she's better off without you. How
can I?

ANATOL. Something of that sort. Tell her she
won't be losing so much.

MAX. Yes . . .

ANATOL. There are hundreds of better-looking
men . . . men better off.

MAX. Handsomer, richer . . . and cleverer.

ANATOL [*half humorously*]. I shouldn't exaggerate.

At this point the waiter shows in the MIMI *in
question. A lovely lady.*

WAITER. This way, Madame.

She doesn't seem to be in the best of tempers.

MIMI. Oh . . . so here you are!

ANATOL [*cheerfully*]. Here we are. [*He takes off
her wrap with much tenderness.*] Let me.

MIMI. You're a nice one, aren't you? I looked up
and down...

ANATOL. A good thing you hadn't far to come.

MIMI. If you say you'll be there for me you ought
Hullo, Max. Come on... let's feed.

There's a knock at the door.

MIMI. Come in! What's he knocking for?

It is the WAITER *again, expectant of his orders
which* ANATOL *gives him...*

ANATOL. Bring supper.

MIMI *sits at the table and, cat-like, fusses he*
appearance.

MIMI. You weren't in front.

ANATOL [*with careful candour*]. No... I hac
to ...

MIMI. You didn't miss much. It was precious dull

MAX. What was on before the ballet?

MIMI. I don't know. I go straight to the dressing
room and then I go on the stage. I don't bothe
about anything else. Anatol... I've a bit of new
for you.

ANATOL [*his brow wrinkling a little*]. Have you
my dear? Important?

MIMI. Myes:.. may surprise you a bit... praps

The supper arrives ... oysters first.

ANATOL. Well... I've some for you, too.

MIMI. Wait a second. It's no concern of h i s.

*This with a cock of the head towards the well
mannered, unconscious waiter.*

ANATOL. You needn't wait... we'll ring.

The waiter departs. Supper has begun.

A FAREWELL SUPPER

ANATOL. Well?

MIMI [*between her oysters*]. I think praps it will surprise you, Anatol ... though I don't see why it should. Praps it won't ... and it oughtn't to.

MAX. They've raised your salary!

ANATOL [*watching her*]. Tsch.

MIMI [*ignoring this levity*]. No ... why should it? I say ... are these Ostend or Whitstable?

ANATOL. Ostend ... Ostend.

MIMI. I d o like oysters. They're the only things you can go on eating and eating ...

MAX [*who is doing his full share*]. And eating and eating and eating.

MIMI. That's what I always say.

ANATOL. Well ... what's this news?

MIMI. D'you remember something you once said?

ANATOL. Which of the hundreds?

MIMI. Mimi ... oh, I remember your saying it ... The one thing I can't bear is deceit!

ANATOL, *not to mention* MAX, *is really taken aback.*

ANATOL. What!

MIMI. Always tell me the whole truth before it's too late.

ANATOL. Yes, I meant ...

MIMI [*roguish for a moment*]. I say ... suppose it was!

ANATOL. What d'you mean?

MIMI. Oh, it's all right ... it isn't. Though it might be to-morrow.

ANATOL [*hot and cold*]. Will you please explain what you mean?

71

ANATOL

MAX [*unheeded*]. What's this?

MIMI [*meeting a fierce eye*]. You eat your oysters, Anatol, or I won't.

ANATOL. Damn the oysters!

MIMI. You go on with them.

ANATOL. You go on with what you were saying. I don't like these jokes.

MIMI. Now didn't we agree that when it came to the point we weren't to make any fuss but . . . ! Well . . . it has come.

ANATOL [*bereft of breath*]. D'you mean . . . ?

MIMI. Yes, I do. This is the last time we have supper together.

ANATOL. Oh! Why . . . would you mind telling me?

MIMI. All is over between us.

ANATOL. Is it!

MAX [*unable to be silent longer*]. Admirable!

MIMI [*a little haughty*]. Nothing admirable about it. It's true.

ANATOL [*with trembling calm*]. My dear Mimi . . . please let me understand. Some one has asked you to marry him?

MIMI. Oh . . . I wouldn't throw you over for that.

ANATOL. T h r o w m e o v e r !

MIMI [*with her last oyster*]. It's no use, Anatol. I'm in love . . . head over ears.

> MAX *goes into such a fit of laughter that choking follows, and he has to be patted on the back.*
> ANATOL *does the friendly office, somewhat distractedly.*

72

MIMI [*very haughty indeed*]. There's nothing to laugh at, Max.

MAX. Oh ... oh ... oh!

ANATOL. Never mind him. Now ... will you please tell me ... ?

MIMI. I a m telling you. I'm in love with somebody else and I'm telling you straight out like you told me.

ANATOL. Yes, but damn it ... w h o ?

MIMI. Now, my dear ... don't lose your temper.

ANATOL. I want to know.

MIMI. Ring the bell, Max, I'm so hungry.

MAX *recovering, does so.*

ANATOL. Hungry ... at such a moment! Hungry!

MAX [*passing back to his chair, says in* ANATOL's *ear*]. Ah ... but it'll be the first supper she's had to-night.

The waiter arrives, ANATOL *rends him savagely.*

ANATOL. And what do y o u want?

WAITER [*perfectly polite*]. You rang, sir?

MAX. Bring the next thing.

While the plates are cleared ANATOL *fumes, but* MIMI *makes casual conversation.*

MIMI. Berthe Hoflich is going to Russia ... it's settled.

MAX. Letting her go without any fuss?

MIMI. Oh ... not more than a bit.

ANATOL. Where's the wine? Are you asleep to-night?

WAITER. Beg pardon, sir ... the wine [*he points it out under* ANATOL's *nose*].

ANATOL. No, no... the champagne.

The waiter goes out for that and for the next course. As the door shuts on him...

ANATOL. Now then... will you please explain?

MIMI. Never take a man at his word! How many times have you told me... when we feel it's coming to an end, say so and end it calmly and quietly?

ANATOL [*with less and less pretence of self-control*]. For the last time...

MIMI. He calls this quietly!

ANATOL. My dear girl... doesn't it occur to you that I have some right to know who...?

MIMI *hasn't let her appetite be disturbed; and at this moment she is relishing the wine, her eyes closed.*

MIMI. Ah!

ANATOL. Oh, drink it up... drink it up!

MIMI. Where's the hurry?

ANATOL [*really rather rudely*]. You generally get it down quick enough.

MIMI [*still sipping*]. Ah... but it's good-bye to claret, too, Anatol. It may be for years, it may be for ever.

ANATOL [*puzzled*]. Oh... why?

MIMI [*with fine resignation*]. No more claret for me... no more oysters... no more champagne! [*At this moment the waiter begins to hand the next course.*] And no more filets aux truffes! All done with now.

MAX. Oh... what a sentimental tummy! Have some?

MIMI [*with gusto*]. I will.

A FAREWELL SUPPER

MAX. You've no appetite, Anatol.

The waiter having served them disappears once more, and once more ANATOL *plunges into trouble.*

ANATOL. Well, now . . . who's the lucky fellow?

MIMI [*serene and enjoying her filet aux truffes*]. If I told you you wouldn't be any the wiser.

ANATOL. But what sort of a chap? How did you come across him? What does he look like?

MIMI [*seraphic*]. He's a perfect picture of a man.

ANATOL. Oh, that's enough, of course.

MIMI. It's got to be. [*She re-starts her chant of self-sacrifice.*] No more oysters . . . !

ANATOL. Yes . . . you said that.

MIMI. No more champagne!

ANATOL. Damn it . . . is that his only excuse for existence . . . not being able to stand you oysters and champagne?

MAX. He couldn't live by that.

MIMI. What's the odds as long as I love him! I'm going to try throwing myself away for once . . . I've never felt like this about any one before.

MAX [*with a twinkle*]. Anatol could have given you an eighteenpenny supper, you know.

ANATOL. Is he a clerk? Is he a chimney-sweep? Is he a candlestick-maker?

MIMI. Don't you insult him.

MAX. Tell us.

MIMI. He's an Artist.

ANATOL. Music-hall artist?

MIMI [*with dignity*]. He's a fellow-artist of mine.

75

ANATOL. Oh . . . an old friend? You've been seeing a lot of him? Now then . . . how long have you been deceiving me?

MIMI. Should I be telling you if I had? I'm taking you at your word and speaking out before it's too late.

ANATOL. How long have you been in love with him? You've been t h i n k i n g things . . . haven't you?

MIMI. Well . . . I couldn't help that.

ANATOL [his temper rising fast]. Oh!

MAX. Anatol!

ANATOL. Do I know the fellow?

MIMI. I don't suppose you've ever noticed him. He's in the chorus. He'll come to the front.

ANATOL. When did this affair start?

MIMI. To-night.

ANATOL. That's not true.

MIMI. It is. To-night I knew it was my fate.

ANATOL. Your fate! Max . . . her fate!

MIMI. Yes . . . m y fate. Why not?

ANATOL. Now . . . I want the whole story. I've a right to it. You still belong to me, remember. How long has this been going on . . . how did it begin? When had he the impudence . . . ?

MAX. Yes . . . I think you ought to tell us that.

MIMI [impatient for the first time]. Oh . . . this is all the thanks I get for doing the straight thing. Suppose I'd gone like Florrie with von Glehn. He hasn't found out yet about her and Hubert.

ANATOL. He will.

MIMI. Well, he may. And then again he mayn't.

But you wouldn't have. I know a thing or two more
than you do.

For proper emphasis she pours out another glass
of wine.

ANATOL. Haven't you had enough?

MIMI. What . . . when it's the last I shall get?

MAX [*with a nod*]. For a week or so.

MIMI [*with a wink*]. Don't you think it. I'm
going to stick to Carl. I love him for himself alone.
H e won't badger and bully me, the dear! .

ANATOL. You and he have been carrying on under
my nose for . . . how long? To-night indeed!

MIMI. Don't believe it if you don't want to.

MAX. Mimi . . . tell the truth. You two won't part
friends unless you do.

ANATOL [*recovering some complacency*]. And then
I've a bit of news for you.

MIMI. Well . . . it began like this . . .

Once more the waiter, with the champagne this
time. MIMI *stops very discreetly.*

ANATOL. Oh, never mind him.

So she gets ahead, but in whispers, till the intruder
shall have departed, which he does very soon.

MIMI. A fortnight ago he gave me a rose. Oh, so
shy he was! I laughed . . . I couldn't help it.

ANATOL. Why didn't you tell me?

MIMI. Start telling you those sort of things! I
should never have done.

ANATOL. Well?

MIMI. And he hung round at rehearsals. It made
me cross at first . . . and then it didn't.

ANATOL [*viciously*]. No, I'm sure it didn't.

MIMI. Then we began to have little chats. And then I began to take such a fancy to him.

ANATOL. What did you chat about?

MIMI *tries the champagne now.*

MIMI. Oh . . . things. He got expelled from school. Then he went into business, and that wasn't any good. Then he thought perhaps he could act.

ANATOL. And never a word to me!

MIMI. And then we found out we used to live close to each other as children. Just fancy!

ANATOL. Most touching!

MIMI [*simply*]. Wasn't it?

ANATOL. Well?

The champagne (one fears it is) has an instant effect. She becomes a little vague and distant.

MIMI. That's all. It's my fate. You can't struggle against your fate, can you? Can't . . . struggle . . . against . . .

She stops suddenly. ANATOL *waits for a minute, then . . .*

ANATOL. But I've not been told what happened to-night.

MIMI. What happened . . .

Her eyes close.

MAX [*with fine effect*]. Hush . . she sleeps.

ANATOL. Well, wake her up. Take that wine away from her. I want to know what happened to-night. Mimi . . . Mimi!

She wakes up, refreshed apparently.

MIMI. To-night? He told me he loved me.

ANATOL. What did you say?

MIMI. I said I was awfully glad. And I mustn't play the silly fool with him, must I? So it's good-bye to you.

ANATOL. It's him you're considering, not me.

MIMI [*with friendly candour*]. I don't think I ever really liked you, Anatol.

ANATOL. Thank you. I'm happy to say that leaves me cold.

MIMI. Don't be nasty.

ANATOL. Would you be surprised to hear that I hope to get on very well without you for the future?

MIMI. Really?·

> ANATOL *throws his belated bomb.*

ANATOL. I am in love, too.

> *And it is received by* MIMI *with the indifference of scepticism.*

MIMI. Think of that!

ANATOL. And have been for some time. Ask Max. I was telling him when you came in.

> *She smiles at this in the most irritating way.*

MIMI. Yes ... I'm sure you were.

ANATOL [*piling it up*]. She's younger and rather prettier than you.

MIMI. I'm sure she is.

ANATOL. And I'd throw six hundred and seventy of your sort into the sea for her. [*But* MIMI, *not in the least impressed or distressed, laughs loud.*] You needn't laugh. Ask Max.

MIMI. If I were you I should have invented all that a little earlier.

ANATOL [*aghast*]. But it's true. I haven't cared that much about you since . . . ! You've been boring me till I could only stay in the room with you by sitting and thinking of her. I've had to shut my eyes tight and think it was her I was kissing.

MIMI [*as comfortable as ever*]. Ditto to that, my dear.

ANATOL *takes a nasty turn.*

ANATOL. Well . . . that's not all. Say ditto to t h i s if you can.

She notices the change in his tone, puts down her wine-glass, and looks squarely at him.

MIMI. To what?

ANATOL. I could have told you all you've been telling me months ago. And weeks ago I could have told you a good deal more.

MIMI. D'you mean . . . ?

ANATOL. Yes, I do. I have behaved very badly to you . . . dear Mimi.

MIMI *gets up outraged.*

MIMI. Oh . . . you cad!

ANATOL [*grateful for the abuse*]. And only just in time, too . . . it seems! You wanted to get there first, did you? Well . . . thank God, I have no illusions!

But MIMI *has gone to collect her things: her hat, her cloak. And she puts them on, too, not waiting a moment.*

MIMI. Oh . . . it only shows!

80

ANATOL. Doesn't it! Shows what?

MIMI. What a brute a man can be!

ANATOL. A brute ... am I?

MIMI. Yes, a brute ... a tactless brute. [*For a moment she gives him undivided attention.*] After all ... I never told you *that*.

Abysses open!

ANATOL. What!

MAX. Oh, never mind!

ANATOL. Never told me what? That you and he ...

MIMI [*with most righteous indignation*]. And I never would have told it you. Only a man could be so ... unpleasant!

> *Heaven knows what might happen,* ANATOL *so twitches with rage and amazement. But the timely calm waiter saves the situation with yet another course.*

WAITER. I beg pardon.

ANATOL. Oh, go to ... ! [*He swallows the word, and recovers a little.*]

MIMI. Ices!

> *And, pleased as a child, she goes back to her chair to begin on hers.* ANATOL, *in his turn, is deeply shocked.*

ANATOL. Can you eat ices at a moment like this?

MAX [*starting on his too*]. Yes, of course she can. It's good-bye to them for ever.

MIMI [*between the spoonfuls*]. No more ices ... no more claret ... no more champagne ... no more oysters! [*Then, as she gets up to go.*] And thank

81

goodness . . . no more Anatol. [*But on her way to the door she notices on the sideboard the cigars. She helps herself to a handful. Then turns with the sweetest of smiles.*] Not for me. They're for h i m!
She departs.
MAX. I said it'd go off all right.
ANATOL *is speechless.*

VI
DYING PANGS

DYING PANGS

One spring afternoon it is growing dusk in ANATOL's *room, though through the open window the broad expanse of sky still shines clear and blue.* ANATOL *and* MAX *come in from a walk.*

MAX. I didn't mean to come up with you.

ANATOL. But don't go.

MAX. I shall be in the way.

ANATOL. I'm not sure she'll come.   Three times out of four she won't.

MAX. I couldn't stand that.

ANATOL. She has excellent excuses.   I dare say they're sometimes true.

MAX. Three times out of four.

ANATOL. Hardly that!   Max, never, never be the lover of a married woman.   There's nothing deadlier.

MAX. Except being her husband.

ANATOL. I've been in this mess ... how long? Two years?   More.   It was two years last Easter that ...

MAX. What's gone wrong?

ANATOL, *who has taken off neither coat nor hat, who still carries his stick in his hand, flings himself into a chair by the window.*

ANATOL

ANATOL. I'm weary of it. I wish... oh, I don't know what I wish.

MAX. Go abroad for a bit.

ANATOL. What's the good?

MAX. Wouldn't that bring it to an end quicker?

ANATOL. It might.

MAX. I've seen you through this sort of thing before. And the last time, how long did it take you to make up your mind to have done with that silly girl who had never been worth worrying about at all?

ANATOL. D'you think things are dead between us now?

MAX. That wouldn't matter... death doesn't hurt. But dying pangs do.

ANATOL. Job's comforter! You're quite right though.

MAX. Talk it over if you like... that helps sometimes. Not to bother over the whys and wherefores, but just to diagnose the case.

ANATOL. You'd like a cheerful ten minutes, would you?

MAX. Well... if you knew what a face you've been carrying round and round the park with you this afternoon.

ANATOL. She said she'd be there.

MAX. You weren't sorry she wasn't. You couldn't have looked as glad to see her as you did a couple of years ago.

ANATOL [*jumping up*]. It's true. But why... why? Have I got to go through it again...

86

this cooling ... cooling ... growing cold? It's a perfect nightmare.

MAX. Run away then ... go abroad. Or else make up your mind to tell her the truth.

ANATOL. What is the truth?

MAX. That you're tired of her.

ANATOL. Tell a woman that sort of truth only because you're weary of telling lies! A pleasant job.

MAX. No doubt you'd both of you do anything rather than face the brutal facts. But why?

ANATOL. Because we still don't thoroughly believe in the brutal facts ... that's why. Even in this dull, dying autumn of our passion, there come to us days of spring ... brighter than any we've ever known. You never so much want to be happy with a woman as when you know that you're ceasing to care for her. And when the happy moments come, we don't look too closely at them either. We only feel so ashamed ... we mutely apologise for having doubted ourselves and each other. Love's like a candle flame ... it flickers highest when it's going out.

MAX. And the end's in sight often much sooner than we think. You can date the death of some love affairs from the very first kiss. But a man may be on his deathbed and swear he's never better.

ANATOL. Not I, worse luck. In love affairs, my friend, I have always been a valetudinarian. Very likely I knew that I wasn't so ill as I thought ... I felt so much the worse for that. I've sometimes fancied I have a sort of evil eye... turned inwards... to wither my own happiness.

MAX. A most rare and distinguished deformity.

ANATOL. You're welcome to it for me. Lord... how I've envied lucky, careless devils, who can be supremely happy in the passing moment. I've never valued a thing when I had it.

MAX. Often they don't know they're happy.

ANATOL. But they needn't feel guilty afterwards.

MAX. Guilty?

ANATOL. She and I knew well enough, didn't we, that though we might swear to love each other till death and after, yet the end of it all was never so very far off? Then why didn't we make the most of our time? For we never did. We're guilty of lost opportunity.

MAX. Oh, my dear Anatol... these dragged-out affairs are very bad for you. You're too quick-witted for them.

ANATOL. Am I?

MAX. Haunted by the past and afraid of the future... why, your one chance of happiness is to keep the present, at least, clear and clean and forgetful. Be a little stupid about it if you must.

ANATOL. Yes... yes.

MAX. But you jumble past, present, and future together till I don't think you know which you're living in. All you think of to-day is your yesterday's remorse for the sins that you mean to commit to-morrow.

ANATOL. And that's not half the nonsense it sounds.

MAX. Thank you. But we must all talk our share of platitudes too ... so here goes for mine. Anatol, pull yourself together ... be a man.

ANATOL. Max ... you can't keep a straight face as you say it. Besides, I don't think I want to pull myself together. What a lot one loses by being a Man! There are a dozen ways of being an interesting invalid, and a fellow can choose his own. But there's only one way of being in rude health ... and that's such a dull one. No, thanks.

MAX. Vanity!

ANATOL. Now for a platitude about vanity.

MAX. No. My only concern is that you won't go abroad.

ANATOL. I may. But it must be at a moment's notice. I hate planning things. I particularly hate packing, and looking up trains, and ordering a cab, and ...

MAX. I'll do all that for you.

Suddenly, as if in response to some instinct,
ANATOL *turns to the window and looks out.*

MAX. What is it?

ANATOL. Nothing.

MAX. I beg your pardon. I forgot. I'm off.

ANATOL. Max ... at this moment I feel more in love with her than ever.

MAX. You probably are more in love with her than ever ... at this moment.

ANATOL. Then don't order the cab.

MAX. But the boat-train don't leave for an hour and a half. I could send your luggage on after.

ANATOL. Thank you so much.

MAX. Now I must make a good exit... with an epigram.

ANATOL. Please.

MAX. Woman is a riddle...

ANATOL. Oh, really!

MAX. Wait, that's only half of it. Woman is a riddle... says a man. What a riddle would Man be for women... if they'd only brains enough to want to guess it.

ANATOL. Bravo.

> MAX *bows to his applause and departs.* ANATOL *is more restless than ever. He paces the room. He goes to the window, where he can now hear some violinist practising in the room above. He lights a cigarette and sits down to wait as patiently as may be. But he hears a sound in the hall. He jumps up and goes to the door as it opens to admit* ELSA. *She comes in a little furtively. She is dressed as a smart rich woman should be, but she is rather heavily veiled.*

ANATOL. At last!

ELSA. Yes... I'm late.

> *He quite tenderly puts up the veil to kiss her. After that she takes it off, her hat too.*

ELSA. I couldn't come before.

ANATOL. You might have let me know. Waiting does get on one's nerves. But you can stop a bit.

ELSA. Not long, darling. You see, my husband...

> *He breaks away from her almost rudely.*

DYING PANGS

ELSA. My dear ... can I help that?

ANATOL. No, you can't. There it is ... we may as well face it. Come to me.

He is by the window and tries to draw her to him, but she hangs back.

ELSA. No, no ... some one might see me.

ANATOL. It's too dark ... and the curtain hides us.

She slips into his arms.

ANATOL. I wish you hadn't to go so soon. I've not seen you for two days. Then you only stayed ten minutes.

ELSA. Do you love me so?

ANATOL. Do I not? What aren't you to me? If I could have you here always ...

ELSA. I'm glad.

ANATOL. Sit by me. [*He draws her close beside him.*] Where's your hand? [*He holds it and kisses it.*] That's the old man upstairs playing. Plays well, doesn't he?

They sit together there in the twilight, listening.

ELSA. Dear one!

ANATOL. Think if we were in Italy now ... in Venice!

ELSA. I've not been to Venice since I was there for my honeymoon.

ANATOL *shrivels.*

ANATOL. Need you have said that?

ELSA [*with a gush of remorse*]. Darling ... but I've never loved any one but you. No ... not ... not my husband.

ANATOL [*in some agony*]. Please do try and forget

91

that you're married . . . just for thirty seconds. Can't you obliterate everything for a moment but ourselves?

> *She apparently does, and there is silence. Then a clock strikes and* ELSA *looks round quickly.*

ELSA. What's that?

ANATOL. Elsa . . . never mind. Forget everything but me.

ELSA [*turning back to him all the more tenderly*]. Haven't I forgotten everything but you . . . for you?

ANATOL. Oh . . . my dear . . . my dear!

> *He kisses her hand and there is silence again. Then the lady says, very tentatively, almost tremulously . . .*

ELSA. Anatol . . .

ANATOL. Yes, darling.

> *She makes a half serious little face at him as a sign that she really must be off. He won't understand.*

ANATOL. What is it?

ELSA. I simply m u s t go.

ANATOL. Must?

ELSA. Must.

> *He gets up . . . goes right away from her.*

ANATOL. Very well.

ELSA. Oh . . . you are difficult.

ANATOL. Difficult! I sometimes think you want to drive me mad.

ELSA. And this is the thanks I get!

ANATOL. Thanks! What do you expect thanks

for? Don't I give you as much love as I get? Is it worth less to you than yours is to me? Why thanks?

ELSA. Don't you owe me just a little gratitude for the sacrifice I've made for you?

ANATOL. I don't want sacrifices. If it was a sacrifice... then you didn't love me.

ELSA. Not love you! I'm an unfaithful wife for your sake... and you say I don't love you.

ANATOL. I didn't say so, Elsa.

ELSA. Oh... when I've done... what I've done.

ANATOL. What you've done! I'll tell you all that you've done. Seven years back you were a pretty gawky girl, weren't you? Your people got you married... because that's the thing to do with pretty gawky girls. Then you went a honeymoon in Venice... you liked that well enough.

ELSA [*indignantly*]. I didn't.

ANATOL. Oh, yes, you did! You were in love... more or less.

ELSA. I wasn't.

ANATOL. He was, then. I'm sure he petted you nicely... anyhow, you were his little wife. Then back to Vienna... and after a bit to boredom. Because you'd grown a pretty woman by now... and, really, he's a precious fool. So you learned to flirt ... harmlessly enough, no doubt! You tell me I'm the only man you've ever really loved. I can't prove it... but let's say that's so. It flatters me to believe it.

ELSA. You call me a flirt.

ANATOL. I do. Did you never indulge in that sensual hypocrisy?

ELSA. Oh . . . you're unjust!

ANATOL. Am I? Then real temptation came. You played with it . . . you were longing for a romance. For you grew prettier than ever . . . and your husband more of a fool. He was getting fat too . . . and ugly. So at last your conscience yielded. You coolly looked round for a lover, and chanced to hit upon me.

ELSA. Chanced to hit upon . . .

ANATOL. Yes . . . if it hadn't been me it would have been the next man. You thought you were unhappily married . . . or at least not happily married enough. You wanted to be . . . one calls it l o v e d. Of course, it was just a flirtation between us at first . . . we skated quite skilfully over thin ice. Till one fine day . . . what was it . . . ? one of your friends looking happier than usual . . . the sight of some merry little baggage in a box at the theatre. Well, and why shouldn't I? . . . said you. And you took the plunge. Leaving out fine phrases . . . that's the story of this little adventure.

> *She does not look at him, but in her voice is shame and reproach.*

ELSA. Oh . . . Anatol, Anatol!

ANATOL. Well?

ELSA. You don't mean it.

ANATOL. I do.

ELSA. That's what you think of me.

ANATOL. I'm afraid so.

DYING PANGS

ELSA. Then I'd better go.

ANATOL. I'm not keeping you.

And she does go ... quite as far as the door.
But there she lingers.

ELSA. You want me to.

ANATOL. My dear! Two minutes ago it was you
that were in such a hurry.

ELSA *looks up in some relief.*

ELSA. Darling ... you know I can't help that.
My husb ...

He suddenly flashes round on her.

ANATOL. Elsa.

ELSA. Yes.

ANATOL. You do love me? Say so.

ELSA [*tears in her eyes*]. Do I? Good heavens!.
what better proofs can I give?

ANATOL. Shall I tell you?

ELSA. I love you with all my heart.

ANATOL. Then don't go. Don't go back home.
Come away somewhere with me. Let me have you
all to myself.

ELSA. Anatol!

ANATOL. Isn't that obviously the thing to do?
How can you go back to him ... loving me with all
your heart? How could I ever have let you? We've
been taking it all as a matter of course. But don't
you see that it can't go on ... it's impossible. Elsa,
dear, come away with me ... you must. We'll go
wherever you like. To Sicily? Very well ... further
then. I'll go as far as you like, Elsa!

ELSA [*blankly*]. My dear Anatol!

95

ANATOL

ANATOL. No one to take you from me ever again. Far away, dear ... we two ... belonging to each other.

ELSA. Go right away?

ANATOL. Yes ... anywhere.

ELSA. But ... my dear Anatol ...

ANATOL. Well?

ELSA [*with a sort of puzzled blandness*]. Where's the need?

ANATOL. Where's the ... !

ELSA. Why go away ... when we can see each other here almost as often as we want?

ANATOL *takes a long look at her and then smiles queerly.*

ANATOL. Yes ... almost. True ... there is no need.

ELSA. You didn't mean it, did you?

ANATOL. Did I?

He turns away from her. She follows him prettily.

ELSA. Are you still angry?

The clock chimes again. He turns back with the utmost politeness.

ANATOL. I'm sure you must go.

ELSA [*a little flustered*]. Oh dear! ... I didn't know it was so late. Till to-morrow. I can come at six.

He helps her with her things.

ANATOL. Please do.

ELSA. Not going to kiss me?

ANATOL. Of course!

He kisses her.

ELSA [*encouragingly*]. Things'll look brighter to-morrow.

ANATOL. Good-bye.

He takes her to the door, where she stops and looks up, all sweetness and charm.

ELSA. Kiss me again.

He looks at her hard for a minute, then very deliberately does so, and she slips away.

He turns back and savagely exclaims...

ANATOL. She asked for that kiss. And it makes her another cheap woman at last... [*Then to himself in the glass*] And you're a fool... a fool!

VII
THE WEDDING MORNING

THE WEDDING MORNING

Note ... In Vienna, of course, a man's clothes for a wedding are what we should call evening dress. It also appears that on such occasions, to every bridesmaid there is a groomsman, whose business it is to provide her with a bouquet.

It is a brilliant winter morning; the lately risen sun shines straight into ANATOL'S *room.* ANATOL *stands on the hither side of his bedroom door, which is a little open. He is listening. After a moment he closes the door very softly and comes back into the room. He looks nervous and rather puzzled. He sits down on not the most comfortable chair with a fretful sigh. Then he gets up to ring the bell. Then he sits down again. His costume is the strangest mixture of early morning and overnight that ever was: a dressing jacket and dress trousers, slippers, and a scarf round the neck; but he looks bathed and shaved, and his hair is brushed.* FRANZ, *his man, answers the bell, and, not seeing him, is going into the bedroom.* ANATOL *jumps up and stops him, more by gestures than with his voice, which he hardly raises above a whisper.*

101

ANATOL. Here, where are you going? I didn't see you.

FRANZ. Did you ring, sir?

ANATOL. Yes ... bring some breakfast.

FRANZ. Very good, sir.

And he is going for it.

ANATOL. Quietly, you idiot. Don't make such a noise. [FRANZ *is quiet, and apparently comprehending. When he is well out of the room,* ANATOL *makes for the bedroom door again, and again listens.*] Still asleep!

> FRANZ *comes back with the light breakfast, which he puts on a table by the fire, saying, very comprehendingly indeed* ...

FRANZ. Two cups, sir?

ANATOL [*with a look at him*]. Yes. [*Then he can hear a bell ring, and he jumps.*] There's some one at the door. At this time in the morning! [FRANZ *goes out again as quietly.* ANATOL *looks around, out of the window, at the bedroom door, then doubtfully at the teacups, and says* ...] I don't feel in the least like getting married.

> *In bursts* MAX, *in the best of spirits;* FRANZ *behind, looking as if he ought to have stopped him.*

MAX. My dear fellow!

ANATOL. Tsch!... don't talk so loud. Get another cup, Franz.

MAX [*at the table*]. Two cups here already.

ANATOL. Get another cup, Franz, and then get out.

FRANZ *obeys with discretion.* ANATOL *is very fretful.*

ANATOL. What are you doing here at eight o'clock in the morning?

MAX. Nearly ten!

ANATOL. Well ... what are you doing here at ten o'clock in the morning?

MAX. It's my wretched memory.

ANATOL. Don't talk so loud!

MAX. I say ... you're very jumpy.   What's the matter?

ANATOL. Yes ... I am very jumpy.

MAX. But not To-day.

ANATOL. Oh ... what is it you want?

MAX. You know your cousin Alma's to be my bridesmaid at the wedding.   About her bouquet....

ANATOL [*with rather sulky indifference*]. What about it?

MAX. I forgot to order it and I forgot to ask her what colour she's wearing.   What do you think ... white or red or blue or green?

ANATOL. Certainly not green!

MAX. Are you sure?

ANATOL. You know she never wears green.

MAX. How do I know?

ANATOL. Don't shout!   It's nothing to be excited about.

MAX [*a little exasperated*]. Do you know what colour she will be wearing at your wedding this morning?

ANATOL. Yes ... red or blue.

MAX. Which?

ANATOL. What does it matter?

MAX. Damn it . . . for the bouquet.

ANATOL. You order two . . . you can wear the other in your hair.

MAX. That's a silly joke.

ANATOL [*his head on his hand*]. I'll be making a sillier in an hour or two.

MAX. You're a cheerful bridegroom . . . I must say!

ANATOL. Well . . . I've been very much upset.

MAX. Anatol . . . you're hiding something.

ANATOL [*with great candour*]. Not at all.

From the bedroom rings a female voice, loud and clear.

THE VOICE. Anatol!

In the silence that follows MAX *looks at* ANATOL *in something more than surprise.*

ANATOL [*casually*]. Excuse me a minute.

He goes and gingerly opens the bedroom door. A pretty pair of arms appears and rests upon his shoulders. In answer to the embrace, for a moment his head disappears. He shuts the door then and returns to his scandalised friend.

MAX. Well really, Anatol!

ANATOL. Let me explain.

MAX. If this is how you begin your married life . . . !

ANATOL. Don't be an ass.

MAX. I'm not a moral man myself . . . but hang it all!

ANATOL. W i l l you let me explain?

MAX [*looking at his watch*]. Hurry up then ...
your wedding's at half-past twelve.

ANATOL. So it is!

*He sits silent for a moment; then slowly
begins ...*

ANATOL. Last night I was at my father-in-law's
... my future father-in-law's.

MAX. I know that. I was there.

ANATOL. So you were ... I forgot. You were all
there. You were all very lively. There was lots of
champagne. A lot of you drank my health ... and
Sophia's health.

MAX. I drank your health ... and her health ...
and wished you both happiness.

ANATOL. So you did. Happiness! Thank you
very much.

MAX. You thanked me last night.

ANATOL. They kept it up till past twelve.

MAX. I know. I kept it up.

ANATOL. They kept it up till really ... I thought
I was happy.

MAX. Well ... that's enough about that.

ANATOL. That fellow Sophia was in love with as a
girl ...!

MAX. Young Ralmen?

ANATOL. Silly young ass ... writes verses! Sort
of fellow who seems to be everybody's first love and
nobody's last.

MAX. Hadn't you better come to the point?

ANATOL. I didn't mind his being there ... it rather

amused me. We broke up about half-past twelve, didn't we? I gave Sophia a kiss ... and she gave me a kiss. No ... she gave me an icicle. My teeth just chattered with it as I went downstairs.

MAX. Well?

ANATOL. There were three or four of them still on the doorstep ... and they wished me happiness all over again. And Uncle Edward was quite drunk and would insist on kissing me. And Professor Lippmann sang a comic song ... in the street. Then Sophia's first love turned up his coat collar and went off ... on the tiles. And then somebody ... I forget who that was ... said of course I'd spend the night under Sophia's window. Damn nonsense ... it was snowing! And after a bit they'd all tailed off ... and there I was alone.

MAX [*to express some sympathy*]. T-t-t!

ANATOL. Alone, in the cold and the snow! Great big flakes ... perfectly beastly.

MAX. So what did you do?

ANATOL. So ... I thought I'd go to the ball at the Opera.

MAX. Oho!

ANATOL. And why not?

MAX. Now I'm afraid I understand.

ANATOL. Not at all! There I stood in the cold and the snow ...!

MAX. Teeth still chattering.

ANATOL. It was b e a s t l y cold. And it suddenly came over me ... made me perfectly wretched ... that I wasn't going to be a free man any more.

Never more a jolly bachelor! Never to go home again without some one asking where you've been. I'd had my last night out. I'd been in love for the last time.

MAX. Get on.

ANATOL. They were in full swing at the Opera. I watched for a bit. Oh . . . that swish of a silk petticoat! And don't a girl's eyes shine through a mask? It makes her neck look so white. Then I just plunged into it all. I wanted to breathe in the sound and the scent of it . . . to bathe in them.

MAX [*consulting his watch again*]. Time's getting on. What happened then?

ANATOL. Was I drunk with champagne at papa-in-law's?

MAX. Not a bit.

ANATOL. I got drunk with that dancing . . . mad drunk. It was m y Opera ball . . . given on purpose to say good-bye to poor bachelor me! I say . . . you remember Katinka?

MAX. Green-eyed Katinka!

ANATOL. Tsch!

MAX *points to where the voice came from.*

MAX. Is that Katinka?

ANATOL. No, it just isn't Katinka. Green-eyes was there, though! And a pretty, dark girl called . . . no, never you mind about her. Do you remember the tiger-lily girl that Theodore . . .? Lisa! I didn't see Theodore . . . but we didn't look far for him. I could tell them all through their masks. I knew their voices . . . I knew their ankles. One girl I wasn't sure about. And whether I was running after her or she after me...? But something in the way she swung her shoulders...! And we met and we dodged, and at last she caught me by the arm... and then I knew her right enough.

MAX. An old friend?

ANATOL. Can't you guess? When did I get engaged? It's not more than two or three months ago. That meant the usual lie... Going away for a bit... back soon.

MAX points again.

MAX. Lona?

ANATOL. Tsch!

MAX. What... not even Lona?

ANATOL. Lona right enough... don't fetch her in yet. We went and sat under a palm. Back again ... she said. Yes... I said. When?... she said. Not till last night. Why haven't you written... where on earth have you been? Off the map... I said... but I'm back again, and I love you still. And don't I love you still?... she said. And the waiter brought the champagne. We were very happy.

MAX. Well... I'm blessed.

ANATOL. Then we got into a cab... just as we used to. She put her head on my shoulder. Never to part she said... and went to sleep. We didn't get back till seven. She's still asleep... was, when you came.

The story over, he sits contemplating the world generally with puzzled distress. MAX *jumps up.*

THE WEDDING MORNING

MAX. Anatol ... come to your senses.

ANATOL. Never to part! And I've got to be married at half-past twelve!

MAX. Yes ... to somebody else.

ANATOL. Isn't that just like life? It's always somebody else one gets married to.

MAX. You ought to change ... you've not much time.

ANATOL. I suppose I'd better. [*He studies the bedroom door doubtfully, and then turns to his friend.*]

ANATOL. You know ... looked at in a certain light this is pathetic.

MAX. It's perfectly disgraceful.

ANATOL. Yes ... it is disgraceful. But it's very pathetic, too.

MAX. Never mind that ... you hurry up.

> *At this moment the door opens and* LONA *first puts her head round it and then comes in. A handsome shrew. She is still in her fancy ball dress; the domino thrown over it making an excellent morning wrap.*

LONA. Oh ... it's only Max.

MAX. Only Max.

LONA. Why didn't you tell me? ... I'd have come in before. How's Max ... and what do you think of this ruffian?

MAX [*feelingly*] I think that's just what he is.

LONA. I've been crying my eyes out for him for months. And all the time he's been ... where have you been?

ANATOL [*with picturesque vagueness*]. Over there.

109

LONA. Didn't he write to you either? But now I've got him safe, he doesn't get away again. Never to part, darling! Give me a kiss.

ANATOL. No . . . really.

LONA. Max doesn't mind [*taking his chin between finger and thumb, she secures her kiss*]. What a face! Look pleasant. Let's all have breakfast and be happy.

> *She settles herself most domestically at the little table and begins to pour out tea.* ANATOL *looks on miserably.*

ANATOL. Certainly.

MAX. Lona, I'm afraid I can't stop . . . thanks very much. [*Then glancing at the wretched* ANATOL.] And I really don't see . . .

LONA. What don't you see?

MAX. Anatol ought . . .

LONA. What ought Anatol?

MAX. Anatol, it's high time that you . . . that you . . .

LONA. High time for what?

MAX. He ought to dress.

> LONA *surveys him in his queer costume without any disapproval.*

LONA. What's the hurry? We'll stop at home to-day.

ANATOL. My dear . . . I am afraid I can't.

LONA. You can if you try.

ANATOL. I'm asked out.

LONA. You send a message and say you can't go.

MAX. He must go.

ANATOL [*with desperate inspiration*]. I am asked to a wedding.

LONA. Oh ... that don't matter.

ANATOL. But it does matter. I'm ... what you might call the best man.

LONA. Is your bridesmaid in love with you?

MAX [*who has followed these efforts encouragagingly*]. We won't go into that.

LONA. Because I am ... so he'd much better stop at home with me.

ANATOL. My dear child, I m u s t go.

MAX. He really m u s t.

ANATOL. For a couple of hours.

LONA. Sit down, both of you. How many lumps, Max?

MAX *thinks it tactful to obey.*

MAX. Three.

LONA [*to* ANATOL, *with a fond smile*]. How many lumps, darling?

ANATOL. I ought to be gone now.

LONA [*with loving severity*]. How many lumps?

ANATOL *sits down helplessly.*

ANATOL. You know I always take two.

LONA. Cream or lemon?

ANATOL. You know I take lemon.

LONA. Lemon and two lumps of sugar. Those are his principles.

MAX. I say ... I must be off.

ANATOL. No ... no ... no.

LONA. Drink your tea first, Max.

The two drink their tea, unhappily. Then ...

111

ANATOL

ANATOL. My dear child . . . I simply must go and change.

LONA. Good goodness! . . . what time is this silly wedding?

MAX. Half-past twelve.

LONA. Are you asked,-too?

MAX. Yes.

LONA. Who's the man?

ANATOL. No one you know.

LONA. But who? Not a secret, is it?

ANATOL. The whole thing's a deadly secret.

LONA. With a best man and bridesmaids? Non-sense.

ANATOL [*explicit*]. You see . . . his people . . .

LONA. You're both dear boys . . . but you are telling lies.

MAX [*with dignity*]. I beg your pardon.

LONA. God knows what it's all about, but it doesn't matter. You go where you like, Max . . . Anatol stops with me.

ANATOL *is getting desperate.*

ANATOL. I tell you I can't. The man's my best friend. I must get him married.

LONA [*prettily to* MAX]. Shall I let him go?

MAX. Dear Lona . . . I think you'd better.

The tension is a trifle relieved, but . . .

LONA. Where's it to be?

ANATOL [*very uneasily*]. What do you want to know that for?

LONA. I'd like to go and look on.

ANATOL. You mustn't do that.

112

LONA. I must have a look at your bridesmaid, Anatol. Best men marry bridesmaids, don't they? I can't have you getting married...so make up your mind to that.

MAX. What would you do if he did?

LONA [*with perfect simplicity*]. Forbid the banns.

ANATOL. Would you now?

LONA. Or I might make a scene at the church.

MAX. That's commonplace...I shouldn't do that.

LONA. No...one ought to invent something new.

MAX. Such as...?

LONA. Turning up at the wedding...dressed like a bride too! That'd be striking.

MAX [*drily*]. Very! I must go.

His decisive getting up encourages ANATOL.

ANATOL. Look here, Lona...I simply must change. I shall be late!

In comes FRANZ *with a bouquet swathed in its tissue paper.*

FRANZ. The flowers, sir.

LONA. What flowers?

Wherever ANATOL *may wish his man, he does not send him away, so* FRANZ, *though not without a sly look at* LONA, *repeats politely* ...

FRANZ. The flowers, sir.

ANATOL *takes them silently, and* FRANZ *departs.*

LONA. Still got Franz, have you? You said you were going to get rid of him.

MAX. And I almost think you'd better, Anatol.

LONA. Let's see.

MAX. It's the bouquet for his bridesmaid.

    LONA *detaches one wrap of the paper. Orange blossoms!*

LONA. It's a b r i d e' s bouquet!

ANATOL [*with great readiness*]. Well, I say ... if they haven't sent the wrong one! Franz ... Franz!

    He carries it off.

MAX. And the wretched bridegroom has got his!

    ANATOL *serenely returns.*

ANATOL. I've sent Franz back with it.

MAX. And I really must go.

    He kisses LONA's *hand and is off.* ANATOL *catches him half through the door.*

ANATOL. What the devil shall I do?

MAX. Confess.

ANATOL. How can I?

MAX. I'll come back soon.

ANATOL. Do ... for goodness' sake.

MAX. But what colour will your cousin be in?

ANATOL. Blue ... or red.

MAX. Damn!

    ANATOL *most unwillingly shuts the door on him, for no sooner has he than* LONA *is round his neck.*

LONA. Thank goodness he's gone ... darling.

ANATOL. Darling!

LONA. Be nicer than that!

ANATOL. I said Darling.

LONA. Must you go to this silly wedding?

ANATOL. I'm afraid I must.

LONA. Shall I drive with you to the church?

ANATOL. Better not. I'll see you in the evening. You've to go to the theatre.

LONA. I'll send and say I'm ill.

ANATOL. I wouldn't. I'll come and fetch you. Now I m u s t dress. Lord...look at the time! Franz! Franz! [FRANZ *is there.*] Have you put out my things?

FRANZ. Your wedding things, sir?

ANATOL [*very steadily*]. Yes...the things in which I always go to weddings.

FRANZ. I will see to it, sir.

ANATOL. After the theatre then...that's settled.

LONA. And I thought we'd have such a jolly day.

ANATOL. Don't be childish. Jolly days have to give way to more important matters.

        LONA *is round his neck again.*

LONA. I love you dreadfully. I don't know what's more important than that.

ANATOL [*as he removes her*]. Then you'll have to learn.

  FRANZ *passes through from the bedroom saying...*

FRANZ. Everything's ready, sir.

ANATOL. Thank you. You've a lot to learn yet.
Into the bedroom he goes, and his talk—or rather his shouting—from there is muffled by the changing of vest and shirt, and punctuated by the tying of ties and slipping in of studs and the brushing of hair. LONA, *left alone, twists discontentedly about the room.*

LONA. Are you really going to change?

ANATOL. I couldn't go to a wedding like this, could I?

LONA. M u s t you go?

ANATOL. Don't let's begin it all over again.

LONA. I shall see you this evening?

ANATOL. After the theatre.

LONA. Don't be late.

ANATOL [*blandly*]. Late! Why should I be late?

LONA. You kept me waiting an hour once.

ANATOL. Did I? I dare say I did.

LONA is still on the prowl.

LONA. Anatol...you've got a new picture.

ANATOL. Yes...do you like it?

LONA. What do I know about pictures?

ANATOL. It's quite a good one.

LONA. Did you bring it back with you?

ANATOL [*puzzled*]. Bring it back!

LONA. From where you went away to.

ANATOL. Of course...from where I went away to! No...it was a present.

Silence for a moment. A shade of half-angry cunning falls on LONA's face.

LONA. Anatol.

ANATOL. What is it?

LONA. Where did you go?

ANATOL. I told you.

LONA. You didn't.

ANATOL. I did...last night.

LONA. I've forgotten.

ANATOL. I went to Bohemia.

LONA. Why Bohemia?

ANATOL. Why not?

LONA. Were you shooting?

ANATOL. Yes . . . rabbits.

LONA. For three months?

ANATOL. Every day.

It sounds as if he were rearing slightly under this spur of cross-examination.

LONA. Why didn't you come and say good-bye to me before you went?

ANATOL. I just thought I wouldn't.

LONA. Tried to give me the slip, didn't you?

ANATOL [*ironically bland*]. No . . . no . . . no . . . no . . . no . . .

LONA. You did try once.

ANATOL. I t r i e d.

LONA [*sharply*]. What's that?

ANATOL. I said I t r i e d I tried hard . . . but it didn't come off.

LONA. I should think not . . . and it's not likely to.

ANATOL. Ha ha!

LONA. What did you say?

ANATOL. I said Ha ha.

LONA. It isn't funny. Glad enough to come back to me that time . . . weren't you?

ANATOL. T h a t time.

LONA. So you are this time. Just a little bit in love with me . . . aren't you?

ANATOL. Worse luck.

LONA. What?

ANATOL. Worse luck.

LONA. Yes ... shout it from the next room. You dare say that to my face?

> ANATOL *sticks round the door a head undergoing a hairbrush.*

ANATOL. Worse luck!

> LONA *makes for it, but it disappears and the door closes. She calls through the crack.*

LONA. What do you mean by that, Anatol?

It is getting to be rather angry chaff, this.

ANATOL. Things can't go on like this for ever.

LONA. What?

ANATOL. They can't go on for ever.

LONA. Can't they? Ha ha!

ANATOL. What?

> LONA, *with some violence, tugs the door open.*

LONA. I said Ha ha.

ANATOL. Shut the door ... shut the door.

> *He slams it to.*

LONA. No, my darling ... you don't get rid of me in a hurry.

ANATOL. Think not?

LONA. I'm sure not.

ANATOL. Quite sure?

LONA. Quite ... quite ... quite sure.

ANATOL. You can't hang round my neck for ever.

LONA. We'll see about that.

ANATOL. Don't you be silly.

LONA. Do you see me giving you up?

ANATOL. When you can't help it.

LONA. When will that be?

ANATOL. When I get married.

The lady, whose eyes are flashing now, begins
to drum the door with her fingers.

LONA. And when will that be ... my precious?

ANATOL [*unkindly mimicking*]. Soon ... my precious.

LONA. How soon?

The drumming grows louder.

ANATOL. Don't bang on the door. This time
next year I may be quite an old married man.

LONA. Fool!

ANATOL. Suppose I get married in a month or
two?

LONA. Some one simply waiting to marry you?

ANATOL. There is ... at this very moment.

LONA. In a month or two?

ANATOL. Or even less.

LONA *laughs with great derision.*

ANATOL. You needn't laugh. I'll be married in a
week.

LONA *still laughs.*

ANATOL. You needn't laugh, Lona!

LONA *tumbles herself on the sofa, she is laughing*
so much. And then ANATOL *walks in, sprucely*
dressed: coated, hatted, and gloved for his
wedding; very self-possessed, moreover, now.

ANATOL. I said you need not laugh.

LONA. When are you going to be married?

ANATOL. At half-past twelve.

She stops very short in her laughter.

LONA. What?

ANATOL

ANATOL. At half-past twelve, my dear.

LONA. Anatol, don't be silly.

ANATOL. I am perfectly serious. I am going to be married at half-past twelve to-day.

>*By this she is taking it in and her breath is leaving her.*

LONA. Are you . . .?

ANATOL. Franz!

>FRANZ *is at the door.*

FRANZ. Sir?

ANATOL. Bring those flowers.

LONA. Anatol . . .!

>FRANZ *brings in the orange blossoms which were n o t sent back.* LONA *understands now. She makes a grab at them.* FRANZ *is too quick for her and secures them to* ANATOL, *and then departs again, suppressing a grin.*

LONA. It's true.

ANATOL [*coolly*]. Quite.

>*But* LONA *is not to be conquered with coolness now. It seems that she is endowed with the very rare faculty of losing her temper. She suddenly makes for* ANATOL *and the bouquet with such complete abandonment of the conventions of civilisation that, with no manly dignity at all, he bolts from her.*

ANATOL. What are you up to?

LONA. You beast . . . you beast.

>*It's the bouquet seems most to excite her and it's that she's after.* ANATOL, *other methods of defending it failing, jumps on a chair at last*

120

and holds it above his head, at which moment
MAX *arrives back dressed for the wedding
too and with his bouquet: pink roses.*

ANATOL. Here ... Max ... help!

The ever-obliging MAX *incautiously comes near.
Pink roses are better than nothing to* LONA, *and
with one snatch she has them from him and
with half-a-dozen pulls she has them in pieces
and under her stamping feet.* MAX *is in agony.*

MAX. Lona ... don't do it! It's my bouquet!
[*He surveys the wreckage.*] Well ... now what shall
I do?

*The lady having sated her natural lust for the
destruction of something—anything; bursts
into violent tears, and abandons herself to the
sofa.* ANATOL *addresses the situation, still
standing on the chair.*

ANATOL. Oh ... she has been riling me! Now
start crying, of course. I told you not to laugh!
Said I daren't run away from her ... said I daren't
get married. So now I shall ... just to spite her.

*In pursuance of which he gets off the chair. But
LONA has another fit of fury ...*

LONA. Sneak! Liar!

*So on he gets again. Again she tumbles down
exhausted. Poor Max meanwhile collects
the remnants of the roses.*

MAX. I say ... look at my flowers.

LONA. I thought it was his. I don't care. You're
as bad as he is!

ANATOL

ANATOL. Do be reasonable.

LONA [*flinging her wrongs to heaven*]. Reasonable! When you treat me like this! But you wait! I'll show you! You'll see!

> *She jumps up and makes for the door. By good luck* MAX *is in the way.*

ANATOL. Where are you going?

LONA. You'll soon see. You let me go!

MAX [*his back to the door and holding tight to the handle*]. Lona . . . what are you up to?

LONA. You let me go! You let me go!

ANATOL. Be reasonable.

LONA. You won't . . . won't you!

> *She then proceeds to wreck the room. The teapot goes into the fire and the teacups out of the window. The table goes over and so do the chairs. A cigar box smashes the new picture and cushions fly around.* MAX *and* ANATOL *do nothing. What can they do? Her work accomplished, the lady has violent hysterics. When the tumult has a little subsided says* ANATOL . . .

ANATOL. Oh . . . I say! Why get married when you can have all the comforts of home without it?

> *And they gaze at the patient awhile.*

ANATOL. She's getting quieter.

MAX. But we must go. And look at my flowers!

> FRANZ *comes in to announce* . . .

FRANZ. The carriage is at the door, sir.

> *And goes out again.*

122

THE WEDDING MORNING

ANATOL. The carriage! What am I to do?

He sits beside the sobbing LONA *and takes her hand.* MAX *sits on the other side, and takes her other hand.*

MAX. Lona! [*he adds over the top of her head to* ANATOL]. Go along ... I'll put it right somehow.

ANATOL. I really must. Poor girl ... I can't ...

He is obviously melting towards the sobbing LONA.

MAX. You go along.

ANATOL. Are you sure you can manage her?

MAX. Yes ... I'll follow you. Watch me when I get there. I'll wink if it's all right.

ANATOL. I don't like it ... poor child. She might ...

MAX *envisages new complications.*

MAX. W i l l y o u g o?

ANATOL. I'd better!

He gets to the door. His heart melts again towards the poor thing who has indeed in the last few minutes sacrificed much to her love for him. He comes back and kisses the top of her head. Then he goes to his wedding. MAX, *left alone with her, perseveringly strokes the hand he holds. She sobs on.*

MAX. Ahum!

LONA *looks up.*

LONA. Where's he gone?

MAX [*securing the other hand*]. Now ... Lona!

Only just in time, for she jumps up.

LONA. Where's he gone?

MAX. You'd never catch him.

LONA. Yes, I will.

MAX. Lona ... you don't want to make a scandal.

LONA. Yes, I do. Where is the wedding?

MAX. Never mind.

She tries to pull away.

LONA. I'm going there!

MAX. No, you're not. What good would it do?

LONA. To be treated like this!

MAX. Doesn't it always happen?

LONA. Be quiet with your beastly philosophy.

MAX. If you weren't in such a temper you'd see that you'd only get laughed at for your pains.

LONA [*viciously*]. On the wrong side of their mouths!

MAX. Think now ... there are lots of good fish in the sea.

LONA. That shows how much you know about me.

MAX. Suppose he were dead or gone abroad? Suppose you'd r e a l l y lost him ... and no help for it.

LONA. What d'you mean by that?

MAX. It's not so much y o u that he's treating badly ... Suppose he leaves h e r some day ... ! Wait and see.

She has calmed a little to the influence of his smooth voice. And now her face lights up with the wildest triumphant happiness.

LONA. Oh ... if I thought he would!

MAX *lets her go.*

MAX. That's nice of you.

LONA. Let me just get a bit of my own back!

MAX. Hell knows no fury like a woman scorned.

124

LONA. No, it doesn't ... does it?

MAX. That is heroic of you. And while you're waiting, can't you avenge your whole sex on every man you meet?

LONA. I will.

She is restored to sanity and self-respect. MAX *looks at his watch rather anxiously.*

MAX. Now I've just time to take you home in a cab. [*He adds half to himself.*] If I don't ... catastrophe for sure! [*He offers her his arm.*] Say good-bye to this happy home.

LONA. Not good-bye.

MAX. Till you come back a goddess of vengeance ... though you're really a rather silly woman. Not but what that answers the purpose as a rule.

LONA. For the present....

Most dramatically, with flashing eyes and curling lip she goes off with him, leaving the wrecked room.

CPSIA information can be obtained
at www.ICGtesting.com
Printed in the USA
LVHW02s2310060918
589445LV00004B/108/P

9 781113 951823